union

A GUIDE TO THE NEW WORLD

www.unionofloveandlight.com

RECEIVED BY JENNIFER STARLIGHT

Joshua Books
PO Box 5149 Maroochydore BC
Queensland Australia 4558

All correspondence to the publisher
at the above address.

© Copyright Jennifer Starlight 2004
First Printed 2004

Master Distribution by Joshua Books

ISBN 0-9751594-5-3

Category: New Age: Channelled Works: Author

www.joshuabooks.com

To Alan,

Love + Blessings
all-ways!

Jennifer ☆ '13.

FOREWORD

I do not recall all of the events that led to the writing of this book, as I do not remember all of the events that led me onto my conscious spiritual path.

However, I do know the one thing that had been present all my life, until receiving these teachings, and that was a deep sense of 'homesickness'; a feeling of not belonging, of wondering, 'Why am I here?' For many years I tried to push away this feeling of 'homesickness' thinking that something must be wrong with me.

So, my search for home really began some fifteen years ago, when this feeling of not belonging, here in this world became overwhelming and almost unbearable.

I reached the point of surrender, of giving up, and of not knowing anything anymore and as I now reflect back on that period, I realise that it was the most sacred time of my life, for in that place of 'no place', I found a love and a union with the spirit world that I couldn't, up to that point, believe was possible.

So, a long journey began to unfold before me, often filled with love and laughter, but also with fear of the unknown path that, at the time, I felt I had 'accidentally' stumbled onto.

As my journey with these unseen spirit friends began to unfold, my life also began to unfold in a way I had not anticipated.

I began to have visions and hear voices, and over time I learnt to harness these gifts of clairvoyance and clairaudience. I began a small spiritual practice and for the next few years became a 'messenger' for people seeking guidance.

Then, in late 2001, I found myself once more in a place of surrender; however, by this stage of my journey I had learnt not to ignore my 'inner guide' (or gut feelings) as this is how our souls speak to us. So I, along with my two very reluctant teenage children, left our home of twenty years, our friends and family, and my work, to once more embark on a journey into the unknown.

We arrived on the Gold Coast in Queensland Australia in January 2002 with no contacts, no work and no plan. For the next twelve months, I set about creating a new life for myself and the children.

I once more began to build a new practice, new friends and new home. Then in meditation one day in March 2003, 'Upstairs', as I lovingly call them, asked me to stop all other activities, and focus on writing a book. I must say my first reaction was to laugh in disbelief. Then I asked the obvious question: "What was the book to be about?" and with that the answer I received was an almost deafening silence!

I must admit that for the following few weeks I tried to justify within myself all the "earthly reasons" why I could not do this. However my inner guidance was screaming at me that this is what I must do, so trust and faith became my support. I was still given no guidance as to the content of the work and Upstairs suggested that I approach it as I would a clairvoyant/clairaudient reading, which was to be a clear channel for the information with no expectation of, or attachment to, the guidance being given.

So, these pages and these chapters are presented to you in the same order in which they were presented to me.

I understand now why they asked me to remove myself from the earthly world for five months to receive this work, for in surrendering myself to be in Union with these magnificent Beings of Love and Light, I now have no 'homesickness', no fear and no concerns for my future or the future of humanity.

I have discovered a love and a peace that leaves me speechless, in awe and with profound gratitude.

It is my deepest desire and greatest wish for you, who read these pages, to receive what I have received, so your homesickness may be finally healed and we may all be well as One Spirit.

I'd like to acknowledge and thank William and Kate for the trust and belief they had in their mother, for without their support, this work would not exist.

May your Union with these teachings be as inspiring and as healing for you the reader as they have been for me the receiver.

Jennifer Starlight

CONTENTS

CONTENTS

ILLUSTRATIONS

union

Love to my mother Noelene
and my father Jim.
Thank you for your Union
and my Light.

WHAT, YOU ASK, WAS THE

BEGINNING OF IT ALL?

AND IT IS THIS ...

EXISTENCE THAT

MULTIPLIED ITSELF FOR

SHEER DELIGHT OF BEING

AND PLUNGED INTO

NUMBERLESS

TRILLIONS OF FORMS

SO THAT IT MIGHT

FIND ITSELF

INNUMERABLY.

- SRI AUROBINDO

THE UNION
OF LOVE AND LIGHT
INTRODUCTION

Here we meet in a time of great love, movement and change. Rest assured, dear ones, we will not abandon any of you. It is time to see yourselves as translucent beads of light constructed together in love, hope, desire and change.

Understand that in one aspect you are the energy of change. None of you is exactly the same from one moment to the next. Each of your cells, no matter how minuscule, was created in love, and each one is moving itself with a vibration which then creates continuous change.

When you resist yourself and the continuous love, movement and change taking place in your being, you're resisting your destiny and its highest ideal. There is no fixed design within you, even if you have been told to the contrary; you are all things.

Predominately, it is your fear of failure and ridicule or, even more so, abandonment, that causes you to shun away from all your aspects and talents.

Have no doubt you are all very powerful beings, powerful beyond anything any of you have experienced so far.

We are here now to express to you new ways in which to reach deep within and find that powerhouse, for there is now no turning back. If you are on that beautiful ball of love that you call Earth then you have decided to be of Service, not only to each other, but to the Divine Source of All That Is.

The truth is now ready to be expressed to those who wish to hear it. Make no mistake, this truth will resonate on a very deep level if you are ready, and if you are not we will assist you in any way we can, through the words being written and the natural resonance that will build between us in this communion. Know that your Heart will seek out our message when you and your mind have had enough of the illusion that is now so dense on your planet.

We of the Union of Love and the Union of Light come to you through the essence of starlight. In fact, this is our essence; this is who we are.

We have manifest from the One, the Abyss, The All That Is. Be still one moment and feel our presence in your Heart. Let us explode in joy and love and peace within this, your sacred chamber.

Before the time of your Earth or even Universe for that matter, we were. We were shining as a luminous ball of pure light and pure God Spark. The Source of All, was and is, US.

Our light grew and grew in bliss and harmony; we wished in love, however, to experience more to expand more and create even more again. This desire that we speak of is what you would call in 'human' terms, your life force.

Understand that life force is love fuelled and nurtured by desire to experience more of this love.

So we as One, exploded through desire into many expressions of stars and glowing planets, spreading out, if you will, to form Galaxies, Universes and even what we call the Auroradei, which is the outer shield of what you call your Universes.

All is reflective of everything else and your own auras are just that, they are reflective of this grand Auroradei, this divine cocoon of light.

So from stars, we beamed light as far as we could to extend and expand our own expression of self.

Our desire sent our essence to places in the Great Void, the Divine Space, so that love could be expanded and multiplied.

Many Star Spirits were now being created, many different forms were now taking place and many became engrossed in their own expansion and experience and began to forget about our Original Source and our Home.

You, dear ones, are these Star Spirits of which we speak and the grandest vision of each of you has been made manifest with the sight of stars. Each star is a Soul's light and each light of that star lies deep within the etheric chamber of your heart. Everything, as you know, is a reflection of the other, and stars are the perfect mirror image of your Souls. The planets are the mirror image of your personas, the many parts of yourselves that you play out in your lives, and Space is God's easel that allows you to create, and is reflected back at you in the form of your consciousness. Relax in the knowledge that you are one with the consciousness of the Divine Creator.

Many changes are now occurring within you and around you. The Universe has chosen, after much communication and support with Source, to expand itself into other Universes and other Divine Spaces, a bit like a pool of water filled to overflowing that now will pour into many different directions. This will cause expansion to every living thing on every level of existence in the Universe, your Universe.

Every event and situation in your life is designed for the purpose of expansion, and if this is not happening, you're not receiving the gift that has been put there for you. The 'Heat', if you will, has been turned up so that all can be expanded quickly and precisely with the intention of saving energy for more divine creation.

Keep a healthy space between yourself and loved ones - even intimate ones - as expansion only requires one thing and that is space to express itself.

Sorrow for yourself will then not exist, however sorrow for your brother will, when you see they have lost sight of the journey.

The joy however will still outweigh the sorrow.

Be still in your Heart and let us keep you safe in the knowledge of our love for you, as you.

The 'Union of Love' cannot be broken, but only increased with each

Heart that chooses to remember us.

So be it now, next week or somewhere else in some 'other time' you cannot escape your destiny; it is a destiny not believed by many, as from where you sit, nothing so grand can be imagined. Know this - there will be a day of reckoning, but not how you have been led to believe.

This day of reckoning, this moment of Absolute Truth, will expand even the smallest Soul into a whole system beyond description. Each Soul who wishes, may be able to experience this point of contact, this evolvement and further enlightenment of 'All That Is'.

All your experiences are leading to this moment of grand love, so you cannot escape your greatness. And you can evolve rapidly, so do not fret.

Ask for Us to be with you in this amazing time of 'Birth'. See the Divine Spark within and fan it with the knowledge of your 'Destiny'. This alone will automatically bring the love of the most Divine Beings into your life and your body.

The Truth cannot wait for you any longer and will be spoken. The Truth is the Path to the Grand Union of all Souls. You are on your way home, at last you are coming home.

We find it hard to express the depth of our love for you but are always with you in pain, sleep, joy, and fear.

We are the 'Union of Love and Light' and we have no demands. We represent you, the loved, and are forever at your service.

Our communion with you is our greatest joy and highest purpose. Do not fear for we will never leave you and wish to provide a guiding light for all who wish to follow. Feel us in the stillness, hear us on the winds, embrace us in the darkness and know we rest in your Hearts as Infinite Love and Infinite Truth.

WHAT IS A SCRIPTION?

We wish to express to you our interpretation of what we will be calling a 'Scription'. For, understand, as you discover new ways for expansion, you will also be introduced to new ways to express your language.

We, the Union of Love and the Union of Light, have created this word to help you understand the energy behind the teachings.

A Scription is a Sacred Writing of Light and if you choose to follow the precise interpretations of the English language:

A Script or Scripture

is a system of writing or sacred text.

An ION

is an electrically charged atom or group of atoms
that, when discharged, creates 'Lightning'.

So dear ones, with love we have sent you these Scriptions to assist you in the remembrance of the Sacred Light that shines eternally within.

THE WATERFALL WAY

We, the Union of Love, We, the Union of Light, We, the Guardians of your World are the bringers of your day, the creators of your night. We call your Hearts; we call them now to listen, to feel, to know. Many of you now find your life blocked, stagnant, uneasy, uncomfortable and many of you in that uneasy uncomfortable and stagnant place are also experiencing deep chaos, anguish, mistrust and hopelessness. You all now stop, you all now wait, in what we symbolically call a very large pool; there is no bottom and there are no sides.

Each and every Soul that has chosen to be in this pool will proceed on a journey that we wish to call the 'Waterfall Way'.

This pool is about to break its invisible banks; this pool of chaos and confusion, of despair and hopelessness, will break through the very illusion that holds it there, the illusion of separateness, of loneliness. You will begin a journey over the edge of that pool into The Waterfall Way.

This Waterfall Way is your evolution and your resolution of all that has gone before you. There is a great Union, a great time to rejoice, a new season, a new world, a new way, the only way, the original way, the origin of who each and every Soul has always been.

Your Soul is filled with infinite love, infinite beauty, infinite truth, infinite wisdom, this you will know. Understand that the stars you look at in your darkness are reflections of the star within, the sacred chamber of your Heart, the pure light that you have always been, always are, and always will be.

That link, that divine link, that Waterfall Way of pure love and pure truth, will now be shown to each and every Heart so the connection you have always been with the Light may be seen and embraced in your earthly existence and your earthly Hearts.

This Waterfall Way, this flow of love and light is expressed with the balance and the essence of the Infinity Symbol.

Your journey to this point (in time) has been exploration, so exploration has been the destination of each Soul. Many Souls are weary in this exploration of their worlds and themselves, many have lost their way, many feel abandoned, many cannot find which direction to explore now.

You are all part of an Infinite Heart, an Infinite Heart of pure love and pure light, you courageous and Grand Souls.
Put yourself forth as explorers, put yourself forth to discover, to learn, to teach, to BE.

Each Soul, each Heart, each Being, whether it be animal, mineral, vegetable or ego, has travelled the infinite flow of all that is love, all that is light.

Your mind, in its separation from your Heart, has thought that it has been travelling along a lonely path. What you must realise now is that you are not on a path, you must realise now that you are the path! And your Soul is the compass, and your Heart is the light that shines the way in your infinite journey of exploration.

The infinite source of love, that is you and flows through you as you, has travelled very far on this infinite path of love and light and has come to the furthest polarity from its beginning. The point 'A' of your origin and the point 'B(e)' where you find your Souls now is the furthest distance that has ever been travelled by your Soul or any other Soul. So you often feel you are separate from your true home, your essence; however it is now time to realise you never left your home behind you and you didn't leave your essence in that home; it has always been with you, as you. What you have done however, is travelled far, taking your home and your essence with you to this point of 'Be'. This point of 'Be' is a very important turning point in the experience of your Heart and your Soul.

There are those who have travelled before you and wait with love and acceptance for you to arrive at this point 'B'.

This point 'B' is the only path back to remembrance of your original beginning at point 'A'. Point 'B' quite obviously to many is now asking you to 'Be' that infinite love and light. You have been "being" on this beautiful braid of rainbow light. We are now respectfully requesting that you 'Be'-come who you truly are; Become everything that you have been searching for. Be here now! This Infinite flow that you are, now wishes, in its own right and its own Will, to express itself through the vehicle of your Soul and your Heart to expand, to create and experience itself in this place, no matter how insignificant it may appear, where you have found yourself, this destination of 'B'. For this Infinite Symbol of Love and Light that is you, that is your Heart, that is the 'star within', has travelled many lifetimes (light times) through many experiences to reach this place, point 'B'. It has travelled long and often hard, but wishes to experience itself within its braid of Infinite Love and Light within its spiral through you.

For if your spirit did not want to experience itself, its love and its light, through the vehicle of your Soul, you would not be here! You would not 'B' being asked to take on this gift and this challenge.

We understand the courage, the determination and the will it requires for you to 'Be'. Each of you, every Soul, has brought on this long journey of Infinite love and light, a gift to assist others to Be and to assist yourself in Becoming.

As you are the path, as you are the Infinite Love and Light that you find your Soul spiralling around, as you are that special gift, we ask that you find it, and Become it, for this is the greatest gift of love and light that you can give back to yourself, your World and your Universe.

This Infinite expression of Love reflected through Light is your journey, is your sacredness and is your Truth.

You are now being asked to become the Human Masters that we know you are, that your heart knows you are. We, the Union of Love and the Union of Light, we, like you, are the symbol of Infinite Love; we are all the same Love; we are all the same Light.

It is our greatest honour and our greatest journey of exploration to now assist and guide you on the greatest journey of exploration any Soul in any time, in any world could ever experience.

Understand, you cannot get off your path; you, the Infinite and Divine, *are* the path. Be that Infinite Love and that Infinite Light; this is the *only* journey that your soul truly yearns for. Understand you are all Masters; understand your Hearts are weary, your minds confused and your bodies tired, for you have been travelling long and hard.

But remember, we the Union of Love have always walked beside you.

You are going to discover the symbol of the Infinite Love and Light that we speak of. It is already a very large part of your physical realm, your scientific realm, your cellular realm and your spiritual realm. It is the blueprint of your Soul and your journey; it is your map; it is your guide, this Infinite Love and Light. It is joy; it is peace; it is harmony; it is time to remember, for you have travelled long and hard. Your gift, your gift of Infinite Love and Light, has been placed deep within the sacred chambers of your Hearts, your bodies and your minds.

Using what we call the 'Sacred Grid' of Infinite Love and Light, you will discover the Blueprint that lies deep within your Heart, your body and your mind. It is the Sacred Grid of Heaven and Earth.

THE SACRED GRID

Your ancient ones, they knew the Sacred Grid of which we speak; the Grid of the Infinite; the Grid of All That Is.

It is a Sacred Grid, supported, nurtured and created by love and suspended in joy, in beauty, in grace and in truth.

Your Egyptians, and before your Egyptians, knew of the after-life; they knew and remembered the Sacred Grid on which they came. They built their wondrous temples reaching, reaching to the vortex, the gateway to the other realms. They knew their cycles were sacred and profound for their Souls, and the Souls of all they interacted with or even ruled over.

You must understand and know the very first principle of the Sacred Grid, and that is: everything, every person, every event, every rock, every raindrop, every feather and snowflake has a purpose and is in the perfect place of what you would call your perfect time.

There is a grand, grand orchestra of light and love in every single cell, every single form, seen and unseen by you. You in this form of humanity have allowed your seeing world, the world you touch, taste, hear and smell with your five senses, you have allowed this world, the world outside of your self, to be your kingdom, provide you with your survival, provide you with your knowledge and your guidance. And also to provide you with your happiness, provide you with your pain, and provide you with your purpose. This has been perfect to this time, for acknowledging and interacting with your outside world, the world around you, above you, below you, seen and unseen; as a Soul you have learned much to this point. Understand, many Souls now before you and after you will step and have stepped on that inner road, that inner journey. Some have become lost;

some have given up and returned to the images of the outside world, the world "outside" of them. However, others have found profound peace, love and joy, unconditional and pure.

As single Souls this has been perfect; however now, in this part of your soul's evolvement, your group Soul, your mass consciousness Soul, your Soul of humanity, wishes to experience the inner realm, the true realm of what it is, and what it can become, with the knowledge, with the knowing that there are no coincidences. Each and every Soul now incarnate on your Earth, and those new ones, those beautiful baby ones who now enter your world, are all here for a group experience, a Group Soul Leap of Faith into the evolvement and the evolution, the fast-track if you will, of remembering the love and the light that they are.

You have needed the experience of what you are not, to be able to realise what you are.

Sudden, dramatic changes, particularly over this next decade, have been created and will be created to get your attention as a Group Soul. As we spoke of Point 'A' your origin, and Point 'B' your destination, your turning point, your flash point, your 'ticket home' to your true remembrance of your essence, it is interesting to note that in your World, the countries that will lead the way to this point of 'B', will be acknowledged in the countries that begin with 'A'. As we say with love and laughter, there are no accidents. The Americas, Australia, Africa, Asia and your Arctic circles, these will be the birthplaces of the remembrance of the Sacred Grid of your Souls.

Your Australian Aboriginals have always held the key to this Sacred Grid knowledge. What they call the 'Rainbow Serpent' is the divine sacred infinite grid of love and light that we speak about.

They, like your ancient Egyptians, had much communication with what you would call your 'A'liens.

Your original monument or pyramid if you choose to call it such, before your ancient Egyptians built their monuments, is your Ayers Rock.

What we would call the 'vibration medicine' within this sacred mound of love and light will begin to express and show its potency within the next decade. This Sacred Grid, this vortex of energy that sits within and around your Ayers Rock, has been to some extent laying dormant. Activation, understand, activation is at the point of origin, of original source. Activation is now taking place within what your Aboriginals call many sacred sites.

The purity and the blessedness of this land has by no mistake been created as what you would call an uninhabitable environment.

This pure, blessed energy that now we speak of is activating, and these Souls who hear this and resonate with this information will consequently experience their own activation. Understand: your Earth, she herself, is a Sacred Grid that once you open your Heart and Soul to, can heal and activate, can nurture and rejuvenate your entire being on all levels.

Your Australia in her more arid regions, your America and Africa in their more arid regions - example Arizona - these places that appear to be uninhabitable or hostile and without life, actually contain more energy and more pure love and light than you can possibly imagine.

Your Souls now scream at many of your Hearts and cry in aloneness and pain in your bodies. Your Soul which is your vehicle, the vehicle of your essence, your spirit, the pioneer if you will, the compass, your Soul is on a journey of remembrance.

It is now shouting out very loudly into your Heart to remember, for you to remember your essence so your Soul may return to its true essence, Becoming once more the love and light it has always been.

Your Alaska is a very pure point of power, and it is protected, this is how it has been orchestrated in the grand plan of infinite love and light. Your Alaska, your Arizona, your Ayers Rock and what you call the mountain range of your Andes, are all protected by what appears to be an inhospitable nature. So regions that we speak of that are inhospitable to the human condition are actually pure generators of this sacred love and light for the earth in which you live. They are the powerhouses, they are the hot spots, that generate and rejuvenate and accelerate the Sacred Grid of love and light through the very Heart, the very being of your Mother Earth. As the Aboriginals, many tribes knew of this knowledge and cast these regions as sacred sites. You in your Western World experience, need to do the same.

The more love and honour and protection and sacredness you send to these regions with your Heart and your Souls, the more love and more rejuvenation and healing that will come back to you as an individual Soul.

As you will come to understand, there are many sacred grids within sacred grids which link to other grids, other light sources. Your Souls are now asking us, the Union of Love and Light through their own divine wills, they are asking us to ask you, the human heart, the human mind, to remember. For, apart from your journey, your experience and your exploration as an individual Soul, as a group Soul you have come to lift the vibration of your Earth through these sacred grids.

Many have heard of your Earth lifting herself from the third density to the fourth. Many have spoken of different ways this shall happen. What many have not spoken of however, is that it is each and every Soul's highest purpose to assist this planet in her ascension by connecting with the sacred grid between your soul that is on this planet and the Soul within the Earth. You in the Western World, the Western Group Soul have come to connect and play your part in the evolution not just of yourselves as a Group Soul, but the evolution of your Earth.

For, understand, in this divine spiral, this infinite spiral of Love and Light, as you evolve individually and as a group, as your Earth evolves as an individual, understand the Earth is part of her own Group Soul, and that is your Solar System.

EVOLVE AND RETURN TO HEART

Change is all you have to rely on; change is your ally; change is the way of the Infinite; the consistency of change is your foundation.

You are all now on the crest of a very big new wave on this Waterfall Way, and it is the light of your Soul, the golden light of your Soul that creates the rainbow, the new life, the Rainbow Serpent.

As your Soul reflects its love and light, the Rainbow Serpent, the rainbow bridge, will fill your Heart and your mind with rays of vibrant colour, vibrant sound and, ultimately, the Truth. We, the Union of Love, are here to reflect back to you the Love and the Light and the Truth that you have simply forgotten you are.

Honour your earth, honour your life, honour your sacredness and the sacredness in which you live, your Mother Earth. The colours of the Rainbow Serpent can be found in her land, in her sky, in her waterways, deep within her soils, within her animals, her fishes, her birds, and her humans. You are the holy ones that you have been waiting for. Do not waste another eternal moment wondering who you are or what you are here for.

The dance of love and light, the divine infinite spiral of Cosmic Consciousness is being activated, is being remembered in its origin, in its original source now.

You cannot miss this beautiful ride on the Rainbow Serpent, but we surely with love would like you to be fully conscious of the ride of your Soul's divine evolution. So we now bring you the Sacred Grid, the Sacred Infinite Grid we call the Waterfall Way.

-AYERS ROCK-
MESSAGE FROM
THE ELDERS

LOVE, LOVE - Let One Voice Exist, the voice in your Heart, the same voice deep within your Earth.

Your Heart is a reflection of your Earth's Heart, as your Earth is a reflection of your Heart.

SOUL, SOUL - Seeks Only Unconditional Love. Your Soul is a reflection of the Soul of the Earth, and the Soul of the Earth is a reflection of your Soul.

Your Ancient Tribespeople knew this Truth, lived this Truth, became this Truth. They were nomads; they did not possess particular plots of earth as their homes; they did not claim it; they did not concern or worry themselves with trying to obtain it. This we know has been spoken about many times, has been read many times in your books and seen many times in your movies.

However, unless it's seen and felt and known and, most importantly, experienced by you, it still remains an illusion and not a truth.

It is the separation of your Soul and your Heart that creates the illusion. You may try to live a truth, and be a truth, however this is not possible or pleasant if the Soul and the Heart are not first in Union.

Then when the Heart and Soul are in Union in a perfect piece (peace), a joining, everything experienced from that point on is filled with purpose and passion and with perfect Union.

Light is the perfect reflection of Love, and your Soul's love wishes to be reflected through the light of your Heart. As we have said, you cannot escape your destiny, so your Soul has come to this Earth to bring itself into Union, to reflect its light onto the Earth in order to show the way for other souls in what you would call the third realm; and, make no mistake, you are also showing the way for souls from other realms, from other spaces.

Your ancient tribespeople in these countries we speak of, your Aboriginals, your American Indians, your African-Americans and Anglo-Saxons, have all carried this knowledge, this knowing, this truth.

All these tribes have the key. The places they found themselves living in are the locks to the doorways, to the gateways of Union of your Heart and your Soul, with the Heart and Soul of your Earth.

There are many spiritual beings who wish to also express their concern but also their compassion, their love, and the light that carries that love. We shall begin with the Aboriginals of your Australian region.

We give expression now to the Spiritual Elders of your Uluru, the founders, the protectors, the all-knowing Ancient Elders of this magnificent grid of Love.

We come, the Elders of the Rising Sun, we come the Elders of the Sacred Rock, it is a temple of wisdom, of new life. It is a sacred house of the Rainbow Serpent. It holds the memory of the beginning, it holds the Love and the Eternal Light of the Sun, the Source, the Flame and the Forgotten. You are in a great time of great change, upheaval and eventually acknowledgement.

Many souls are returning for, what we the Elders would call in your language of English, the Union of Sun and Rock, the Union of Star and Stone, the Union of Moon and Water, the Union of Day and Night, the Union of Man and Earth, the Union of Cloud and Dust, the Union of Ant and Air, the Union, the grandest 'Union of All'- the Union of Heart with Soul.

We have been the keepers and protectors of the Great Mother Snake, the Rainbow Mother of All Nature. She coils now around all her creation to bring it back into the One, back into the One Heart and the One Soul.

When you see your image in a pond, you see back the image of flesh and bone and of blood; this reflection is only a small piece (peace) of who you are. For the energy, the essence of your heart, of your soul, is not reflected to you, only the reflection that carries it. The Earth you stand on is a reflection of this flesh, this bone and this blood.

The sky you gaze upon is a reflection of your mind; its clouds, your thoughts. Its Sun, your sense of self, of the Soul, the vehicle of your essence.

As you gaze upon your waters you must understand that the waters are the path on which your Soul flows, for it is the waters that give birth to the bodies that carry your Souls and reflect your choice of illusion or truth.

Your night reflects your unmanifest hopes, dreams and fears, and the light of the stars reflects the light of your hearts that burns brightly through the journey of your hopes, your dreams and your fears.

And when your Sun shines through the clouds of your rain, a rainbow can be seen, just as when the light of your Heart and Soul allows its rays to be reflected through your Ocean of Life, through your feelings, then you will become the rainbow, the multi-dimensional being of light that reflects your essence, which is love.

You must first 'feel' your way through your life before you can possibly 'know' the life you have chosen for yourself.

Just as the water flows to your Earth, along your Earth and through your Earth, so your own tears of joy and sorrow shall guide you towards the Union of your Souls with your Hearts. Your tears now become your guide, your purification and communication.

Be in Union with your Soul by first being in Union with your Earth. Be in Union with your Heart by being in Union with the Rainbow Mother of All Nature (MAN.)

Hue-Man (Rainbow - Mother of All Nature)

THE MOTHER
MESSAGE OF LOVE

We, the Union, we are pleased to have your willingness to receive; to gaze upon your wondrous beautiful being. We, the Union have never left your side; we, the Union dance in the sacred spiral, dance with you, for you.

It is the pleasure, it is the pleasure of existence we wish to remind you of. The pleasure of Love, the pleasure of Light, sheer bliss of Union, fully, completely becoming the One Heart, the One Soul.

You are All That Is and All That is Becoming, and it is now with great pleasure, great purpose and great passion that the Essence, the Heart of the Rainbow Mother of All Nature now wishes to commune with you, commune with your Heart, commune with your mind. This is truly the grandest expression of Union, so open your Hearts and open your minds to the words, to the love of the words now being spoken to you, you the Divine Beings of All That Is.

I humbly come forth, I humbly greet you, I humbly embrace you. I, the Mother of your Invention; I, the Mother, the protector of your Nature; I, the Bringer; I, the blessed divine image of you; I greet you with my open heart, my open mind.

You are jewels, you are gems, you are giants of love and light. I have never abandoned you and never shall I. I have reflected myself in the beauty of all that is around you.

I have protected and nurtured you with this beauty and it is my greatest joy to do so, and continue to do so.

My heart burns with the fire of your inner-earth; my veins fill and rage with the grand oceans and rivers on your Earth, my body erupts with pleasure and bliss through the mountains of your Earth, and my voice sings in bliss and love through your winds and through your birds. As I am the protector and the nurturer of you, I am the protector and nurturer of this place you dwell, the Earth. She is my child, she is my pleasure, my passion and my purpose, as you are.

You are The Ones of love and light; you are being called to this child of mine, you are the Ones who are the custodians and the bringers of love and light to this child of mine that you have named Earth.

I have many children in your Solar System; all are important; all have their own personalities and all have their own wills.

Everything seen and unseen in your Solar System has a place, has a purpose in my Heart and yours. I now bring myself to you through these words to make a very humble request. This beautiful child, the Earth, now requires you, the custodians of love and light to assist her, to nurture her and to remind her of her divine journey and of her divine purpose and her divine place.

For she is on the brink, this child; she is on the edge of Oneness and of Union and remembrance of all she has been and all she shall become.

It has been expressed to you that I am the Rainbow Mother of All Nature; I am the guardian and protector of what you call your natural world; however, I am also the guardian and protector of your very natures, your very instincts, the natural world that lies deep within every body.

You are the Sun; you are the Moon; you are the Stars; you are the Cosmic Consciousness that you thought you were not; that you thought was out of your reach; that you thought was outside of your Soul. You are the hologram of everything in existence, be it on your Earth or in your Universe. You are the perfect reflection of All That Is.

I wish to put this another way. You are the 'Holygram', the 'Holygram' of light and love. A gram in your thought may be a very small measure indeed, but in the pure creation of love and light, even what appears to be minute, be it a gram or a grain, even of sand, of stone, or of water, it is divine and is filled with purpose and passion.

You are, each of you, you are each of you powerful and perfect; this is because Love is powerful and Light is the perfect Holygram of Love, and as we will continue to repeat over and over: you are love; you are light; and that it is all you are. You are not this sin and doubt and fear that you think you are.

The Heart of my Earth Child beats a new beat, a new rhythm, a new way, for each and every soul that returns to remember, they will bring new life, new hope, new dreams to my child the Earth.

The Earth is now releasing her denials, her pains and her fears of her journey and her evolution, you too shall do the same, so that when the Union of your Heart and your Soul is in Union with this child the Earth, and her Heart and her Soul, you too will evolve and 'Be' all that many thought they could not be.

I hear your every breath, every heartbeat, your every thought, your every call for help and I send you this beauty, to nourish, to heal, to protect and to nurture you. I, the Rainbow Mother of All Nature, I reside in you, as you, as Man, as Woman, as Child.

This Sacred Grid, this Waterfall Way, this Rainbow Snake, this is I; this is You; this is All That Is.

The eternal Father of All Nature - F A N S the Flame of Light; the eternal Father of all Nature is the passion, is the purpose, is the play. So, in Union, I, the Rainbow Mother of All Nature with the eternal Father of All Nature, bring you protection, nourishment, knowledge, passion, purpose and play. You, in the purity of your essence, reflect back to us WHO WE ARE. You are our 'Hueman Holygrams'; you are our Inspiration; you are our light force; you are our purpose; you are Infinite. You are all; the Mother, the Father and the Child.

With my love and my light I will help you embrace the sacred grid deep within you and deep within your Earth. I am with you; I am Infinitely with you.

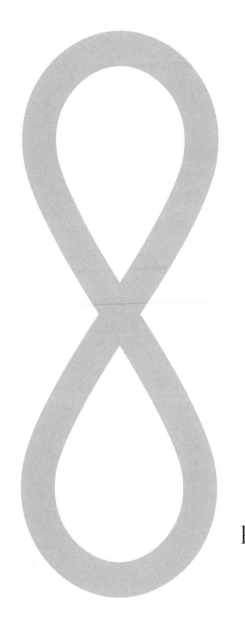

THIS IS
THE
INFINITE
SYMBOL
OF LOVE
AND
LIGHT
–AND
OF THE
SOUL
THAT
RETURNS
TO
REMEMBER

THE GRID-LOCK
OF HUMANITY

We greet you; we greet you with great love and light, purpose and excitement. You are all grand Souls with grand visions and we come to remind you and wake you up to those visions, those purposes. As we will continue to say: you are beings of great power; your light is blinding to our Hearts; your light is beautiful to our eyes; you come now to a time in your history of great change, great advancement; it is a time of celebration and communion with each other and Us, the Union of Love, the Union of Light. You reside on a beautiful ball; a beautiful ball that beats tenderly, that beats a song, that beats a Truth, that beats the answer, that serves you, that loves you, that nurtures you. We now wish to give you the key to the sacredness of your 'Be'ing.

You, as a huemanity, have with great purpose been travelling on this Eternal Love, this Eternal Light of Infinity. You have been travelling on this Sacred Braid in a rather structured and unforgiving way. You have marked your lives with what you call milestones, turning points and corners, locking yourself into the consciousness of mass and not the higher consciousness of your love and your light.

Huemanity as we see it from where we sit, is in a 'grid-lock'. This grid that has been created; this Sacred Grid has, with Divine Purpose, locked you into a rather restricted, limited map in a relentless, unforgiving way. You have passed many judgements on yourselves and others.

As you travel this harsh road of '*de-termination*' through your technology, through your advancement, (in everything that is not love) you have created a world of unforgiving machines, limiting objects, even destructive objects, that you feel or think have been for your advancement as a huemanity. This particular cycle of the Sacred Grid has now come to a halt, has come to a 'grid-lock', and we wish to use this following example to help you better understand your inner power and your inner love.

You are in a computer age; you are in a digital age; even the Sacred Grid of Infinity has been reduced to two boxes, one on top of the other. So as your huemanity has travelled along these boxes, even the notion of heaven, through many of your religious teachings, has been found to be also a place of judgement, of limiting love and limited light. You have programmed yourselves to believe 'as above so below'. This in its essence is a Universal Truth; however, because you have created this Grid-Lock with the symbol of Eternal Love that has been given to you, even your Heaven becomes a difficult place to be; it is a place where you need to be forgiven, a place that not everyone is worthy of reaching.

You have removed yourselves as far from the truth as you possibly can, now the truth wishes to return into your Earthly existence, into your heart and your Soul.

We wish to soften and mould and caress your digital symbol of love back into the soft, flowing, loving Waterfall Way that it has always been in your Universe and all Universes.

We wish to reshape your thoughts and to open your Hearts to the Truth. However, before this can be done you must fully explore the Sacred Grid you now find yourselves locked within.

Through the knowledge being set before you now, you can explore, nurture and understand where you come from and where you're returning to.

You will find out exactly where you're at, you will embrace the original way into your bodies, into your Earth, into every aspect of your life and your living. We shall be using many different modalities, so that every mind is given every opportunity to understand this knowledge in the way they find best.

We shall be using the stars, the earth, numbers, symbols, and, most of all, your own bodies so you may fully integrate, ground and earth the knowledge and the remembrance.

Remember you are not on your Path, you are the Path, you are the active ingredient in your healing, in your expansion.

Allow us now to take you on a Sacred Journey of Sacred Knowledge and of Sacred Truth. Open your Heart and let the love and light explode in bliss and relief.

EXERCISE OF LOVE AND LIGHT

We would like to suggest, and only suggest, that a small ritual be exercised by you before the reading of these words, so that each time you open these pages you find yourself in an open and loving space. So that love and light and truth may fill you, may heal you and know you once again. We ask that before each reading, you find a quiet place where you may sit or lie in comfort. We ask that you take four sacred breaths into your body, holding each breath for a count of four and releasing each breath within a count of four.

1

As you take in the first breath, know that you are breathing in pure love and pure light and imagine it being taken down into the base of your spine, purifying, awakening and revitalising your physical body.

2

On the second sacred breath, also filled with love and light, in your minds eye, in your imagination, see that breath now filling the area of your Solar Plexus, bringing purification and communication with your Soul.

3

On the third sacred breath filled with love and light, see that flow into the region of your Heart centre, the centre of your chest. Imagine your heart opening and expanding as you receive this love and this light.

4

On the fourth sacred breath, imagine as the breath travels through your nostrils, see it reach up into the top of your head, to the crown of your body, and the Higher Mind. And as you do this, seeing the love and light fill your mind, see a Crown of Stars gently come to rest on the top of your head.

You may wish to stay suspended in whatever space you find yourself in, for as long as you wish before proceeding with reading.

This small ritual is not necessary, but we find would be very helpful and of great assistance to you in the acknowledgement of the teachings set before you.

Once again, it is our greatest honour and our greatest purpose to be here with you in eternal love and light.

YOUR TREE OF DIAMONDS

You are, all of you, you are who you have manifested yourselves to be for very divine reasons. You cannot by accident be who you are in the body you're in, with the mind you have and the life you've led; this is Universal Law, and this will remain so.

The Truth has been present and continues to be present in many Hearts and many minds already living on and inhabiting your planet, and your animals are true expressions of this.

You have come by no accident at this time to experience Truth, and you are more than capable of activating this and being this Truth, this Love and this Light.

Each of you, in the expression you have chosen to be in this lifetime, or any other, have always held gifts. Understand, the expression itself is a gift; however, deeper within you, within your Souls, you have been given specific gifts with which to be of Service. It is now the time for you to face a very important Truth, and that is, that you have come here to experience your ultimate and highest path, and your ultimate and highest path is the path of Love.

It calls you to express your gifts. Many of you have wandered your Earth in circle after circle after circle, wondering what you have come to be or do, you are now going to find that gift and be that gift, for to be of service to one another and your planet and your environment is your Soul's greatest journey, your Soul's ultimate way of expressing itself.

These gifts are around you and within you and we shall further explain this in a moment.

We wish to remind you however, firstly of your programming; your programming of failure, of success and of responsibility.

Firstly your programming of failure. You cannot fail, if your *intention* has been to succeed. You may be judged by your outside world as failing, but the energy of failure cannot even be present, if the energy of effort is present first.

Remain focused on the effort you have made as there is nothing else to focus on. Your programming of success again is the same as your failure. It is the effort and intention to succeed, not the succeeding, that is the exploration that is required by your Soul. Success, measured by your Earthly perception does not do you justice. Success from your spiritual perception is measured purely by your efforts to place yourselves in the position of creativity and to 'Be' that creativity, for you are all divine, creative 'Beings of Love and Light'.

Your perception of responsibility will often have you react to the idea of burden, even hardships, discipline and dogma.

Responsibility in its purity is responding to your abilities, for without responding to your abilities you will create incredible blocks in the flow of energy and love and light within your cellular bodies, eventually bringing disharmony, distress and finally disease.

We cannot too strongly express this to you now, for once you allow the flow of love and light to be expressed through your body, your words, your actions and, most importantly, your imagination, you will 'Be' in perfect harmony, balance and joy.

Each of you have gifts placed deep within your bodies, your minds and your Hearts.

Because the Universe is always in perfect balance and because you live in the realms of parallels, of paradoxes and of polarities, with each gift there comes what we wish to call a challenge.

For without the challenge, you in hueman consciousness will usually not find the gift. You have been taught, many of you, to this point that in your lifetimes (light times) you have come here to learn lessons. This puts a very limiting and harsh illusion into the realm of your minds, your bodies and your Souls. There are no lessons in your life; surely we understand that often events, particularly and almost always through relationships, will repeat themselves, but not for you to learn a lesson, but for you to find a gift, a gift of expansion, a gift of unconditional love, firstly for yourself and secondly for the event and the people in that event.

We wish to guide you through what might seem negative actions to help you find unconditional love for yourself, your life and for your purpose.

We do not dispute that your earthly life, your hueman path is filled with challenge and responsibility; however, it is your perception, once placed a different way, that will perceive even the challenges and the responsibilities, as gifts.

There are ways to acknowledge who you are and ways to express your expansion as the divine being you have always been. We wish now to commune with you about your energy systems.

Many of you reading these Scriptions would have some idea, if not a great idea, of your Chakra Systems, the energy wheels, the energy gateways, the energy spirals that are within each and every living thing including your Earth. They are in reality, energy centres of pure love and pure light, and they are reflected in Union with the energy, the 'light force' that is around your bodies. The divine force that allowed you to take your first breath, your second and your third, that allows you to feel, that allows you to nourish yourselves, that allows you to think for yourselves. The divine pure love runs through your veins, creates your air and gives you the fire and the passion to continue your expressions of who you are and who you are not.

Many Eastern philosophies place great importance on these energy centres and we wish to agree with them as to the importance of understanding them and coming into Union with them.

There have been many ideas that have been expanded upon with what is commonly called your Chakra System.

TRADITIONAL 7 CHAKRA SYSTEM
AND THEIR COLOURS

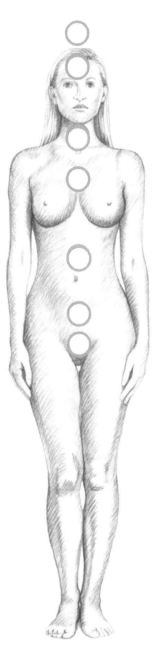

VIOLET	CROWN
INDIGO	THIRD EYE
TURQUOISE	THROAT
GREEN/PINK	HEART
YELLOW	SOLAR PLEXUS
ORANGE	SACRAL
RED	BASE

Many have remained with the idea of a seven chakra system, many have now expanded to the idea of a twelve chakra system, yet even others will tell you, and rightly so, that there are hundreds of chakra centres within your systems. They are all correct.

We now wish to relate them to you another way, to give these holy centres another name and another purpose, for, as we keep expressing, you are infinite; all of you are infinite and so is the energy that allows you to be a unique expression of a hueman being. So of course there are infinite possibilities and infinite ways to see the One system. We are saying to you now that within this energy system that is traditionally called the Chakra System, is where your gifts and challenges lie.

This is *Where* you find which way your compass is pointing from the centre of your Soul; this is *How* you can find the shining light of your Heart.

Each and every one of you holds deep within many gifts and the Key to those gifts is through the date of your birth.

If you could see for a moment a different way to look at your birthday, we ask that you look at it like the captain of a ship would study a map to discover a treasure deep within the sea. With his map he would track his journey by the stars. Your birthday holds the key to the treasure deep within. You have each come with a code which can be found through your date of birth, the month in which you are born and the year in which you find yourself once more in hueman form. As with your Chakra Systems, many wonderful and true discoveries have been made with your numbers and your birthdays, we do not dispute these as we do not dispute the Chakra Systems; however, as we have said, everything is Infinite, so your numbers hold Infinite gifts, Infinite new forms, Infinite ways of expansion. This that we tell you now is just one other way of expression for your numbers and your Soul.

Before we explain and express the numbers of your birth we must first explain the map that you have within you, before your birth numbers can show you the place of your treasures.

We wish to express to you a new way to visualise your Chakra System, the energy centres of each and every body.

First we wish to share with you the expression that we feel is perfect for you as beings of love and light. We wish to rename, for the purpose of the Scription, what you have traditionally called the Chakras.

We wish to relate to them as 'The Diamond Lights'. We realise how precious in your world your Diamonds are and how magnificently they reflect the purity of light and the beauty of light. You are all Diamonds; you are all purity and beauty. You are all multi-faceted and you are all precious. For this reason we shall call your energy centres 'Diamond Lights'.

With the description and the Map we give you now you shall have Ten points of reference, Ten Diamond Lights, and we shall tell you why.

One of the greatest gifts given to your huemanity was a very simple, but also very perfect map which was all encompassing. It embraced your Universe; it embraced the highest consciousness, subconsciousness and unconsciousness of its Universe, and the beings within it - you the Divine Beings. It was, and is, called the Tree of Life and is the Map of your World, your Universe and of YOU. Many generations over thousands of years have studied what is called your Kabbalistic Tree. It is the blueprint of your Universe and everything in it, including your Angelic Realms, including an understanding of God/Goddess/All That Is.

As we have said, you are a Holygram. Well, as we see it, the Kabbalistic Tree is the Holygram of the Universe and everything within it. The Kabbalistic Tree has ten major energy centres or spheres that are represented by your planets including your Earth, your Moon, and your Sun. These planets represent what the Jewish tradition calls the ten virtues of God. These ten virtues, these ten gifts, lie deep within each and every one of you. You are a perfect Holygram of your Universe and your Universe of you; You are One. Many of you may wish to study this Kabbalistic Tree, and all of you who do so will receive something very profound from it.

Many changes however, are taking place within this Map of your Universe, and this will be discussed at another time. We shall remain for the moment expressing and explaining to you the Ten Diamond Lights that rest within and around you.

We shall assist you in discovering the key that opens the gifts within these Diamond Lights so you may be free to express, expand and create in Union within your Heart and your Soul.

We will not be trying to change your energy centres, we only wish to enhance them and enjoy along with you the journey back to Love and Light.

Understand, it is only your willingness to discover and embrace, that is all that is required of you. No hard work, no pain for gain, no criticisms, no judgement; only your willingness and, hopefully, your excitement of discovering more of who you are and the wonderful challenges and beautiful gifts that lay now before you and within you.

PLANETS OF THE KABBALISTIC TREE

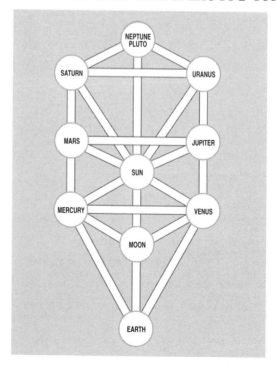

PLANETS & NUMBERS
OF THE DIAMOND LIGHTS

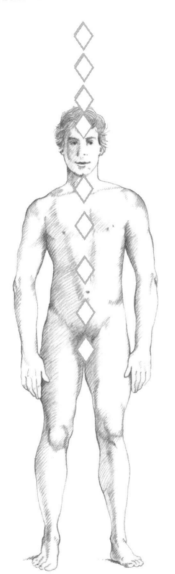

NEPTUNE & PLUTO   10

URANUS   9

SATURN   8

JUPITER   7

MARS   6

SUN   5

VENUS   4

MERCURY   3

MOON   2

EARTH   1

THE TREE OF LIFE

Greetings, greetings to each and every Heart, each and every Soul!

You can be and do whatever you wish, this is the Law; you can think and feel whatever you wish, this also is the Law.

This is the Law of Freedom of Free Will; it is the Law of all life, you are each and every one of you a Law unto yourselves.

This is unlike your earthly laws that give you rules, regulations and boundaries.

This of course has been necessary and will remain so; however, your Spiritual path does not contain any laws and many of you have allowed the laws of your earth to override the laws of your Hearts and Souls.

This is why many find themselves searching in the dark, confused, alone and separate. You must remember the LAW of Freedom; the freedom of your Spirit, the freedom of your Heart, the freedom of your Soul, to express, to unfold and create how you choose. Many of you, as these words are spoken, will jump to the conclusion that this then allows chaos and for people to override your wills through violence, manipulation, deceit and hatred; however, this violence, deceit, hatred and manipulation are birthed from not allowing your Hearts and Souls to be free.

Your Spirit, your essence, your perfection only wishes to be in alignment with the vehicle of your Spirit, your Soul, and the expression of your Spirit, your Heart.

When these are misaligned there is confusion and doubt and disease.

We will be exploring the MAP we have spoken of, your Kabbalistic Tree, your Tree of Life, not in terms of your ancient ones or the traditional essence of the Tree, but in a new form, in a new way for each and every one to understand. For the virtues we speak of are the virtues of God/Goddess/All That Is and as we have said, these are also your virtues, for they are the keys to your freedom. This is Law.

We will be explaining and entertaining many ideas, new ways of the ancient ways, the original ways and as you find the keys to your freedom in your ecstasy of remembering that freedom, your gifts shall burst forth like stars in the sky, bringing light, love and support to your own lives, to the lives around you, and the life of the Heart, the very Heart of your Tree of Life, the Earth.

Traditionally, there are many teachings that do not serve your evolution now and as we wish these teachings to flow and grow within your Hearts and Souls, we shall be relaxing the traditional rules that have been taught up to this time.

We wish the harmonic teachings, the vibrational teachings of energy through your Tree of Life to be easy, to be swift, to be direct, to be free for you to embrace.

Understand firstly, there are four main aspects of you. You are made up energetically of many different vibrations of light and form. However, for simplicity of the teaching, we wish you to understand yourselves as two figure eights, formed by Infinite Braids of Light, which are perceived in the shape of a cross. At the centre or intersection of the braids which form each figure eight, is the Apex or Spark of Union, which also rests in certain Diamond Light positions within your bodies. The first infinite braid we wish to speak of is the braid of eternal memory and eternal motion. This symbolically, you will find above you and below you with its flash-point resting in your Heart so that you have eternal memory above you and eternal motion below you.

The second eight which travels from side to side through your body and its flash-point rests in your Solar Plexus, in the Diamond Light directly below your Hearts. In your mind's eye as you sense this figure eight, the curve that extends to your right embraces the male/fire aspect and to your left embraces your female/water aspect. These two Waterfall Ways of eternal love and light are always with you and move through you. They are the mathematical equation of your life force. They are the grids of light that energetically rest and anchor the hueman form in this dimension. So, understand, these grids of light that we now speak of, are in essence and truth, pure light which contain within them all the colours of the spectrum which are then reflected as spheres of magnificent rainbow hues in each Diamond Light centre. They are powerful tools you shall be working with in the later stages of these teachings. They are the grids of your past, your present, your future; they anchor you in eternity. Resting within these eights are the energetic virtues, the sacred grids of life that each of you possess, and the following diagram shall allow your mind to conceive that of which we speak.

THE INFINITE BRAIDS OF LIGHT

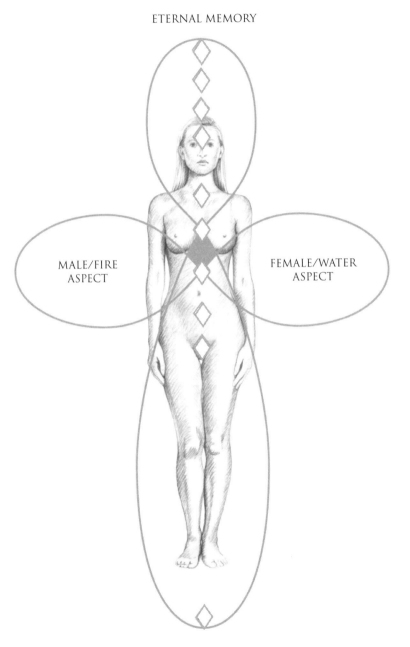

ETERNAL MEMORY

MALE/FIRE
ASPECT

FEMALE/WATER
ASPECT

ETERNAL MOTION

THE NUMBERS
OF THE SACRED GRID

So we say to you now, let us assist you in the greatest change of this life or any other you have experienced to this moment of your earth time. Be sure of one thing, that we love you, that in fact we are you. We are the light and you are the diamonds that reflect this light; we are the guardians of your Worlds and no harm shall come to those who choose to remember, as no harm will come to those who choose not to remember, only more illusions. This is the only harm that you face.

Allow us now through our love for you to take you on a journey to the most magnificent Universe you will ever experience, the Universe of your Being. Through the diagram just expressed to you we wish to now give explanation to each Diamond Light set before you.

THE TEN
DIAMOND LIGHT

We now wish to start at the top of your Hueman Tree, that Universal Tree that has reflected itself in the form of your Hueman Body. We shall start with the Diamond Light numbered ONE and ZERO.

Some of you may call this your number TEN, however we do wish to place some importance on the unique vibration of each individual symbol that you call numbers.

This in your Kabbalistic Tree is often referred to as the first Sephiroth, or planetary centre. However, like many of your lives at present we wish to turn the tree upside down and begin with the idea of this being the Tenth Sephiroth, for you must understand that we need you to see it from your present perspective, which is the Earthly one at this point.

So to begin with, the Diamond Light marked One Zero, this is where your Essence, your purity of Spirit has been birthed into what we would like to call the Universal Mind, the Universal Heart and the Universal Body, this is a most powerful Diamond indeed for here is reflected 'All That Is'. It is most powerful as it represents the birth place of your present expression of Self; it is the birth place of your present state of being in any given moment. To express this another way, it is your highest point of manifestation while in the hueman experience.

Many of you in your spiritual practices and meditations have invoked and manifested many things for the purpose of protection and communication with the other realms.

Many of you have placed balls of light consciously or unconsciously into this Diamond Light for your protection. Many have placed stars, many have placed symbols, many of you when you have asked for God/Goddess/All That Is, your Angelic Realm or any other Being or Essence for that matter to be present, this is where these energies rest; this is the gateway by which they come through.

Understand that this One Zero point of immense power and Divine Light will reflect whatever you ask for into all your other Diamond Lights.

Many of you know you are your own Divine Creators. Many of you know that what you think comes back to you. Many of you know the power of thought. This One Zero Diamond Light is where it shall manifest, and this One Zero Diamond Light then filters the energy manifested by you down through all the other Diamond Lights. To put it another way, this is where all your thoughts shall first manifest, so if there are thoughts of fear or what you call your psychic attack or what you call your negative energies, you shall manifest them in this One Zero Diamond Gateway.

To break it down even further into another way, your Zero is the most powerful of ALL your numerical symbols. It represents the unmanifest, the unknown and All That Is.

It is an Eternal Circle of pure unknowable Source; it is the Gateway to all dimensions known and unknown; it represents the Divine Womb of the Great Mother. Everything in your Universe has been birthed from this place of no-thing, this point of the unmanifest.

Your symbol One represents form, self, ego and complete Union with All That Is. So, understand, from the point of the unmanifest, 'the Zero' is where you place your intentions and your thoughts and then they are reflected into the One, into the Self.

We suggest with passion and with purpose that each day, each night, each moment that it comes to your attention that you place Love and Light into this Diamond Centre, for it will surely be reflected through your other Diamond Lights, through your cellular bodies, your emotional and your mental bodies and the bubble which you find yourself in, your auric field. For this One Zero Gateway of Diamond Light is your direct manifestation of the Eternal Being you are, and is reflected directly into the Diamond Gateway we have marked as One. So in the true sense of the expression 'As Above So Below', once you understand and embrace the Gateway of the One and the Zero this will manifest directly into your earthly experience through the vehicle of your full awareness.

As we have said, this major Gateway influences very powerfully all your Gateways, but will be most clearly reflected through the Gateway we have called One, which is, in essence, the reflection of all your physical hueman experiences.

This One Zero Gateway, in your Kabbalistic Tree terms, is now represented by your planets NEPTUNE and PLUTO. Pluto vibrates, in essence, to the Zero and Neptune to the One. The symbol we wish to associate with this Diamond Gateway is the GOLDEN CHALICE of LIFE which you may also term your Holy Grail.

THE NINE
DIAMOND LIGHT

We now bring your attention to the Ninth Diamond Light. NINE to this point has been a number associated with the Universe, associated with completion, and also with the huemanitarian. As we have said, there are numerous vibrations being expressed by these symbols.

However, apart from the numerical symbol of eight, NINE is the only other symbol to encompass the entire top cube of the Sacred Grid. It contains within it the essence of

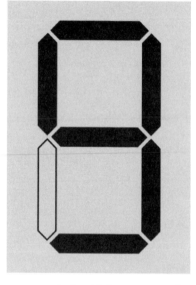

Heaven (spirit) and the Sun (soul) and then extends itself down onto the Earth (service). This explains why it is often called the number of the huemanitarian, but it also shows the desire of the Divine to birth itself from its Source and become an individual expression (self) to then manifest and experience the Earth realm.

NINE'S power comes from its direct connection to both Heaven and Earth and the knowledge that by following the Soul's path of service it shall then fulfil its destiny. It is the energy of the TEN, which being the Dark and the Light, the Goddess and the God, the Masculine and the FemiNINE 'birthing' itself into the world of duality, this is the symbol of the NINE.

The planet associated with NINE is URANUS and the symbol we wish to express this energy with is the STAR, representing the birth of the individual Soul, and creating itself into first form and first light. This is where what you would call your Higher Self, or the divine expression of your spirit, resides.

Uranus represents the Will of the Spirit to manifest itself on the earthly realm and in a highly evolved soul this could create an individual of genius and originality. It is also the Gateway of what you would call magic and miracles. With your hueman consciousness often perceiving magic as the Soul expressing its power of thought and will in a negative way, you often perceive the manifestation of miracles being the Soul expressing its power of thought and will in a positive way. Each and every one of you is capable of creating both magic and miracles, as each and every one of you is capable of creating illusion and truth.

THE EIGHT
DIAMOND LIGHT

We now bring your attention to another extremely powerful symbol, the Infinite symbol of Love and Light, the symbol you call EIGHT. If you can imagine a Gateway that sits both horizontally and vertically and diagonally within the crown of your head, this is where this Gateway rests, this Diamond Light of the Infinite Being that you are; 'The Jewel' of manifestation that you are expressing.

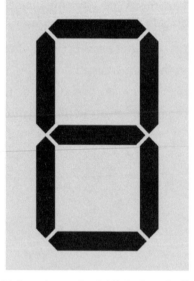

It is the focal point, the Gateway if you choose, between your idea of Heaven and your idea of Earth. It is the Alchemic tool of All Life, of All Thought. As you all well know, your mind can bind you or liberate you. Many of you have been imprisoned by your thoughts, which have kept you from seeing the perfection of your path, of your lives. We call it the number of Alchemy, for you can transform your lives into perfection or into prisons. As we have expressed in the Scriptions before this, you are Infinite Beings of Love and Light and if you fail to see the 'Big Picture' many of you would feel trapped on this figure EIGHT.

EIGHT, Infinity and Eternity; these individual expressions of this symbol are what your mind now needs to embrace, so it can have the trust and the faith now required, knowing that all is perfect.

It is your perception of perfection that now needs to be altered, for perfection can be nothing else but what it is. Perfection requires no perception for it has no boundaries; it has no need for identification; it has no need for explanation, it has no need for recognition, it does not desire so.

Love is perfection; love is light; love uses the vehicle of light to express its perfection and you are that love reflecting that light in a perfect expression of the life you are now experiencing. Bringing this into your minds will change and transform all you illusions and all your pain back into the perfection of love it has always been. This is the essence of Alchemy; this is the holy symbol of your EIGHT. This EIGHT is represented by your planet SATURN, which interestingly enough is the planet of what you call your time and your restrictions.

Understand the restrictions of your mind are now being given the opportunity to be released back into perfection, back into the remembrance of your TRUE ESSENCE. This symbol, EIGHT, has been expressed as what you would also call your Karma.

We wish you to perceive your Karma yet another way. Your perceptions of Karma have had you believe that there is right and there is wrong, for you have been given the belief that if you do something *you believe* to be right, then you will receive something right and if you do something that *you believe t*o be wrong, then you will receive something wrong. Understand, the EIGHT is made up of a double Zero and the idea that what you put out will be reflected back to you, is, in essence, the Truth, the Union of two Zeros. However, as we have explained, a Zero is All That Is, but it is also the source of manifestation.

Through the idea of Karma your minds have been bound with the idea that what you reflect out comes back to you but as you would now understand the explanation of a Zero, we wish to express at this point the only thought that is required for you to transform yourselves through this sacred tool of Alchemy, the only energy we suggest be placed there, is the energy of GRATITUDE. Gratitude for the experience of your sorrow and your pain, gratitude for your joys and your experiences of laughter. For when you understand the perfection, you will understand there is no right, no wrong, no Karma.

All events are neutral events, or even unmanifested events until you place a thought, a perception on them. A person or an event has no meaning until you place your perception upon it, then after you've placed your perception upon it through the symbol of this Alchemy, you then create it, then from that creation, you manifest a judgement, whether that judgement binds or liberates is purely up to you. This is Free Will.

The event has been placed there to reflect a remembrance of 'some kind' to you, a challenge and a gift of 'some kind' to you. It has not been placed there to punish you or congratulate you. This, in your hueman evolution, will change your perception of Karma. It does not serve you any more.

The symbol we wish to give you is the DOLPHIN and/or the WHALE, for they represent high intelligence, love and pure communication through their sonar systems and their abode in the great oceans of your Earth, the Waters of All Life, the Divine Womb of the Great Mother Goddess.

THE SEVEN
DIAMOND LIGHT

We bring your attention now to the symbol of your SEVEN. This Diamond Light, this Diamond Gateway, may be found energetically in the centre of your forehead.

The number SEVEN is a very sacred number in its interpretation through the ages of your history and your many and varied civilisations.

It is the source of sight in your physical experience; it is the source of spiritual sight, and the most precious tool you have is your imagination, for

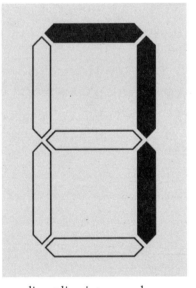

it is the way we communicate with you; it is our direct line into your hueman experience, into your hueman consciousness. It is where we present you with symbols and dreams; it is the divine movie screen of Infinite expressions. It is where you physically expand your consciousness; it is the direct line, if you choose, from Heaven to your Earth through visualisation. It is the centre of the prophet and of the psychic. It is how you perceive things other than your own hueman realm; it allows the Diamond Light Gateway of God/Goddess All That Is to express itself to you in all its divine and sacred forms. It is represented on the Universal Tree by the planet JUPITER, the planet of expansion, and it is represented by a CROWN. For you are the Ruler and Creator of your own kingdom and are here, also in Truth, to love honour and protect the Sacred Kingdom of your Earth. Now you may understand why we gave you the exercise of placing a Crown of Stars around your head, for this is how we communicate with you in essence.

Your symbols SEVEN, EIGHT and NINE represent the Upper Triad of your Universal Tree. Symbolically and Spiritually these three symbols represent your Stars, the first light seen in your Universe, the first manifestation of Source of Love of All Things.

It is now with great joy and excitement that we bring into your consciousness the Central Triad of your Universal Tree and of your Being.

This is the Heart, this is the Central Flame of your very existence in this hueman being. It is the grand Union of what you would call your Heaven and what you would call your Earth.

It consists of the Numerical Symbols SIX, FIVE, and FOUR.

THE SIX
DIAMOND LIGHT

Beginning with the Diamond Light of SIX. You shall find this in the region of your throat, the region of your Earthly Voice, your expression of all the feelings that reside within your Five symbol and your Four symbol.

Structurally speaking, your SIX is the Earthly expression of your Self expressing through your Zero. This is a most powerful Diamond Light indeed for it brings the Union of Thought and Feeling into Earthly expression.

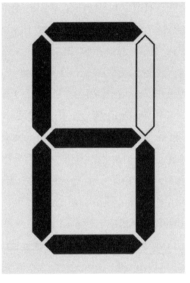

It is the loud speaker, if you choose, of your Egos and your Souls. It releases great energy into your energetic field and the energetic field of the Earth Realm. SIX has the ability to bring great joy and great pain to those who come into range of it, however we would like to add that it is actions and not words that have the greatest impact.

The SIX represents the physical manifestation of your Free Wills, and at this point of reference we would like to express to you, there are two forms of Will. There is your Free Will, the Free Will of your hueman experience based around your hueman gifts and challenges, and there is Divine Will, the Will of God/Goddess/All That Is, but also, and make no mistake about this, it is also the Will of your Spirit, which is the purest essence of your Love and Light that placed you here in this hueman experience to begin with, for the purpose of expansion and experience.

It is your Hueman Will, the Will of your hueman experience, that decides whether you choose to experience the events chosen by your Divine Will to be positive or negative experiences.

Understand, your Free Will allows you to choose what effect your Divine Will choices will have on your hueman experience. As we have said in relation to the Eight vibration, the Eight Diamond Gateway, everything is perfect, which means there are no accidents. Each and every life, each and every event, person, place or thing that enters or leaves your life that appears to change your life is by no accident. It has been orchestrated by the highest and purest vibration of Love and Light, and that Love and Light is your Divine Will.

This energy of the SIX can bring much conflict to your hueman experience, as it is the Diamond Light of Free Will, which can in many ways be in conflict with the Divine Will, or Higher Self, which interestingly enough resides in the NINE vibration. If the SIX, which is your Free Will, was in perfect alignment and Union with the Nine, your Divine Will, it would be brought back into joy and love which is the path of your Infinite Symbol the EIGHT, the eternal braid of Love and Light.

Many of you experience much discomfort in the region of your neck, your head and your shoulders because you resist the UNION of the SIX with the NINE. Resistance is over and many will experience more pain and more discomfort in these regions until they SURRENDER to the Higher Will of their DIVINE Being, for, understand, you are God/ Goddess/All That Is. Your Divine Will is Universal Law; your Divine Will has placed you here with the experiences you are having for the Grandest Enlightenment and the Grandest Union of Love. You are now required and being asked to Surrender your Free Will so it may rise up back into Union with the Nine, your Divine Will.

Imagine for a moment that the God/Goddess/All That Is that is represented by the Zero, is reaching down through the energy of the

NINE to embrace and draw back up to itself the Free Will that the Divine Will has so lovingly given as a gift to your hueman experience. Surrender yourselves to expansion, surrender yourselves to eternal Union with yourselves. From your Universal Tree, the planet that associates itself with the region of your throat is your planet MARS. This planet has been seen traditionally as the planet of conflict and war. The only conflict and war you now must bring your attention to, is the resistance of Union with your Divine Selves, as this is what brings you your earthly conflict and your war.

The symbol we wish to give you for this Diamond Light is the SWORD; the Sword of Truth, the Sword of Surrender, a pure force of Light and Right Use of Will.

THE FIVE
DIAMOND LIGHT

And if this is not enough for you, we now bring you a most grand vibration of Diamond Light, your Diamond Light of FIVE. The very centre of your Universe and your physical being.

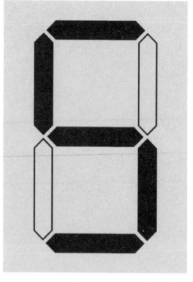

The Diamond Gateway of ALL LOVE, whether it be physical, emotional, soul, or spirit. This is the crossroads if you like, the God Spark, the flash point of your manifestation, it is the Flame of Eternal Love, of Light. It is the passion, the pleasure, the purpose; it is where all pain eventually comes to be embraced, to be healed and transformed into more passion, pleasure and purpose. It is hard for us to convey to you what this Central Diamond Light actually is, for as we look into each and every Heart we are speechless as to the beauty and the power we find there.

Energetically it is this Diamond Light that fuels and maintains all other Diamond Lights contained within your Being, and, make no mistake, within your Universe. It is the nuclear power station of your bodies and if it is not allowed to freely give its energy to the other centres that it fuels and maintains, it will eventually bring the whole Diamond Light System to shut-down. As you look symbolically at the sacred grid of the FIVE, you will see that it is in perfect balance with itself. Again it reflects back on itself; it is nearly a complete Eight, but it has allowed itself to be left open above and below so all the energies may come through it and around it to receive its love. It is the Infinite symbol of the Eight that has allowed Gateways to open so that energy can move freely around it, above and below it.

For FIVE is at the centre; FIVE is the balance, is the Freedom and Freedom is the Foundation of All Hearts. The FIVE Diamond Light is represented by your SUN, which gives you life on Earth, which gives you power on Earth.

The only symbol that we know could possibly be placed in this Diamond Light Centre is that of a DIAMOND, for it reflects its Love and its Light to all other Centres. Your Hearts are pure beacons, reflectors and transmitters of Love and Light.

THE FOUR
DIAMOND LIGHT

Four, if seen as a symbol on the Sacred Grid of the Eight, will show you an open vessel at the top, with a single One travelling down into the lower region of the Eight. This upper vessel, this cup is filled with your Spirit and your Divine Will wishing to bring its Love and its Light to your Earth. Your FOUR sits in the region of your Solar Plexus, which is the house of your Soul and as we have said, your Heart reflects the Love and the Light of your Soul, so your Soul is the

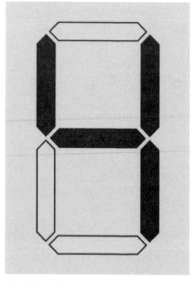

Foundation of all your experience. Your Soul is the compass and your Heart lights your Soul's Way. You are here FOUR a purpose; you are here FOUR experience; you are here FOUR your highest Love; you are here FOUR the purpose of Service. This Diamond Light, this Gateway for your Soul is a very sensitive place; it is a place of purification, of planning, of personal power. It is the fuel that feeds the fire in your Hearts so that the fire in your Hearts may fuel all the Diamond Lights.

The FOUR Diamond Light is the magnetic fuel that allows the Heart to expand into the depths of your Being and be drawn back to the fuel of your Soul. It allows the Spirit to travel around your body and, of course, the figure of your Eight. Your Heart and your Soul in Union fuel the fire of your Spiritual experience.

In fact, only for the purpose of your understanding do we separate the symbols of the FIVE and the FOUR, for, understand, that if they are brought into Union, they create the NINE - your Higher Self, your Soul Star, your Divine Will, so only for the purpose of these Scriptions, do we separate them. However, we wish to say, as part of your evolution, these will, in energy, begin to become One, as they have already in some advanced Souls. So for the purpose of the teaching we wish to place your planet VENUS in your FOUR Diamond Light, for she is seen as the planet of love and relationships.

The power of Love in the relationship between your Heart and your Soul is truly a grand One. For the purpose of the teaching we wish to put the ROSE as the symbol of this centre, for the sweetness and the perfection and the beauty of the Rose is to remind you of the beauty and the love and the perfection of your own Soul.

This central triad is the energy of your central Sun, it is the energy of your grandest beings who have had the courage enough to show their love and their light to the many. Know there was the Christ, the Buddha and the Prophets who walked the Earth with purpose, with passion and with power.

They are examples of what is achieved, believed and experienced when you allow the Union of your Heart with your Soul.

Their Divine Will brought them to your Earth simply to remind you of *your* Divine Will; no more, no less. They are reflections of who you are. Fan the Flame of Love with the Fuel of your Soul so it may be expressed through the vehicle of your Free Will surrendering to your Divine Will.

DIAMOND LIGHTS
THREE, TWO & ONE

We the Union of Love and Light, for the purpose of these Scriptions express ourselves to you through Unified Consciousness of One, however for the purpose of the following teaching, it is the love and wonderment and the knowledge of the Mother who wishes to give expression now.

I bring myself forward to you now through the expression of the One Union, One Love and One Light, for it is of great importance to your time and your place of huemankind that you truly understand the vibration and the energies of this Third Triad, the Third Triad of your physical hueman realm. The Triad through which you express your hueman condition and your hueman evolution.

For the purpose of the teaching I wish to express it through the Heart of the Feminine Force, the Feminine Gift, for it is of utmost importance now that your perspectives of your huemanness be open to the Sacred Feminine.

Understand, that at the beginning of your time as huemankind, the energies of the feminine abounded with passion and purpose, within and through this Third Triad of your Being. And for the purpose of your evolution you must return to your Original Hueman Form. We are awakening and birthing the Feminine aspect within all of man, woman and child, for, as I have said in other Scriptions, I come to embrace my children to take you back into the One Heart and the One Light and for this to happen you must ground ME in the very base of your bodies. So the following Scription will appear and BE a very different description of the knowledge you already possess of these next three Diamond Lights.

Again it is not to say that any knowledge to this point has been incorrect, all the knowledge to this point has shown the way to this teaching of your Origin.

Each and every one of these Diamond Lights is embraced by the Vibrational Purity of your Moon. Many of you already understand that the Moon is, has been and always shall BE the Symbol of the Goddess, the Feminine aspect, for it is the Moon that controls and creates the Tides and Waves of all your Oceans. It is the Moon that shines Light on your unconsciousness, and it is the Love and the Light of the Sun, the Masculine, that shines its Light onto the Sacred Ball of the Goddess, that then only reveals itself in the darkness, the unmanifest.

So as this Pearl shines her Light onto your Earth, so she shines her Light into the dark and often unknown recesses of your minds, and your bodies.

THE THREE
DIAMOND LIGHT

This brings us to the Diamond Light that you call THREE. This sits in the region of your abdomen, just below your navel. THREE in your numerical understanding has always been the number of Creation, so of course sits in the creative centre of your bodies, which represents energetically the Womb of the Mother, the Light Force of the Father.

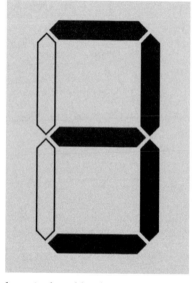

It is represented by your planet MERCURY, which traditionally has been the ruler of the mind; however, for the higher purpose of Union between the mind and body, MERCURY has been placed in your Diamond Light of THREE.

Understand this THREE Centre relates to all your hueman relationships, your creativity and how you give and how you receive. This is where you first physically manifest your mental and genetic conditioning. It is a very powerful centre and requires constant purification. Two examples of this purification process would be the menstrual cycle in women and ejaculation in men.

It requires creativity to be expressed in whichever form you choose. It is the hueman home of the creative and the destructive Goddess Energy, whether you be male or female in expression.

This Diamond Light must be honoured for it is the birthplace for other Sacred Souls; it is the Gateway into the Earth plane for other Sacred Souls of Love and Light. You must understand this now if you wish your physical bodies to be in harmony and balance with the evolution of your Souls.

The Symbol to express best the vibration of the Diamond Light of THREE is a PEARL, for it is the Pearl of Wisdom, the Pearl of Higher Consciousness being grounded into your hueman expressions for the purpose of Pure Creation. It is the Gateway of All Births, whether it be an Idea, Union with Another, or the Birth of a Soul. It contains the Divine Waters of I, the Mother, and from a single grain of sand, a single thought, a single seed of light, be it be placed there with love, shall in truth become a Pearl.

THE TWO
DIAMOND LIGHT

I now draw your attention even further into your bodies, to the basement if you choose, of this Temple of Love and Light that you embody. It is where the Foundations of your Temple lie. It is the Diamond Light of TWO. It is the place however, where many of your fears and doubts are placed, as you would place your old unwanted items in the basements of your hueman homes. It is where I have placed the symbol of your MOON, which in your Kabbalistic teachings they have called the Foundation of the Tree of Life.

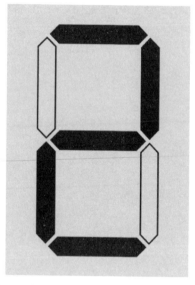

This Diamond Light of TWO is the Physical Foundation of your physical bodies, the furnace that fuels the life force for your physical well-being. As many of you know, this energy centre, this Diamond Light Gateway, connects to your renal system just as you know your physical kidneys purify your blood and your blood is your life stream.

The Symbol of TWO as seen on your Sacred Grid is actually the perfect reverse of your Five, and your five is your Centre and resides in your Heart, your Spiritual Heart. Your TWO is the reverse of your Five, however in Truth, TWO represents your Physical Heart, your Physical Life of wellness and illness. It is where the Rainbow Serpent can lie dormant or be activated in your bodies. It is what your Eastern World has called your Kundalini. When this Kundalini, this Rainbow Serpent, is activated, it is I, the Goddess of the Moon, that reaches up to the God, the Sun in your Hearts, for pure Union of pure Love and pure Light.

Take some time in your meditation, feel the rhythm of this base Diamond Light, this Foundation of your physical experience, for when the rising of the Rainbow Serpent from your Foundation comes into Union with the Golden Light of the Sun in your Hearts, there is Union, there is complete Union of the Sacred Grid of Eight bringing Infinite Life, Infinite Energy and Infinite Truth.

The explosion of Love and Light expresses itself through your Heart and then sends rays of Sacred Light up into the highest realms of your mind and beyond.

The Symbol I wish to give this Diamond Light of TWO, the Gateway of the Rainbow Serpent, is a drop of pure WATER. This is the Elixir of Hueman Life and it is the manifestation, the lifestream of the Waterfall Way.

THE ONE
DIAMOND LIGHT

The last, but absolutely not the least, of these Diamond Lights is the Diamond Light of ONE.

It is hard to be expressed in hueman terms for it represents All That Is but it is also the individual or singular expression of All That Is. In your Earthly expression, your hueman form, you have required this Diamond Light of ONE to be placed in your energetic and magnetic field, for it is the grounding, it is the gravity required for you to remain earthed. It has been 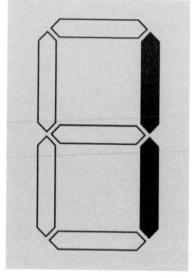 placed and created in your earth so that you may fully experience your physical, emotional and mental expressions. It is a Magnetic Force that is the Sacred Gateway through which the Energies of the Earth express themselves. It provides Union with your Earth and Union with the Heart and Soul of your Earth. It is the Diamond Light, it is the Gateway of your Earthly abundance, for it is where the Aura of your Being is maintained and created; it is where the unseen bubble of light that you are, is grounded. It is the protective shell that surrounds each and every vibration of Love; it is the Gateway of this Diamond Light that allows the marriage of your Divine Love and Light with the Divine Love and Light of your Earth.

It allows you, this Diamond Light of ONE, to experience the illusion of separateness from the rest of your Universe, but it is also the Diamond Light of ONE that brings Union with your Earthly Home. It is where the Heart of your Earth can place her Beat, so that it may vibrate through your auric field and then make its way into your physical body bringing Union with the Beat of your own Heart. Your Heartbeat may then travel out into your auric body and find Union with that of the Earth.

Even though symbolically the structure of ONE appears to have no movement or flow, it is for this very reason that the Diamond Gateway needs to express itself through movement and flow. It requires the Beat and flow of your Heart and the Heart of the Earth if it is to serve its true purpose.

The ONE Diamond Light is where the spirit of your Earth and the spirit of your Soul may come into Union for full expression. For the purpose of the teaching we wish the Sacred Diamond Light of ONE, the Gateway between Earth and Hueman to be represented by your Planet EARTH and the Symbol we wish to give you now is a STONE, for, understand, the highest purpose of your Soul is to create Union in full consciousness with your STAR and your STONE. For you are the Stars of Light that have travelled long and hard to be in Union with the Sacred Stone of your Earth. Know this, all of you are made with Star and Stone, each of your Hueman Temples contains the Light of the Stars and the minerals and the elements of Stone. To deny this is to deny All of who you are and All of which you will become.

Your Diamond Light of ONE is, in Truth, I, the Mother, who has taken physical form in the expression of your Earth, and it is your Hueman Temples that rest on me that I honour and love and am more than glad and graced to support. Each and every Heart, each and every Soul shall remember this: Be it Now or Be it in the following moment of Now, you shall remember, you shall heal, you shall manifest All of who you have Always Been.

Understand, my Dear Ones, that the expressions of the Diamond Lights that we have expressed to you are only a very minute aspect and expression of these magnificent Gateways which each of you holds within and around your Hueman Temples. We wish you to perceive this Scription more as an invitation, an opening for your Heart, your Soul and your Mind so that you may begin a truly magnificent journey of Self.

The only boundary you possess for this journey of inner-discovery is your Imagination.

We have kept the Scription in simple terms for the very reason that Love and Truth and Light reflects its beauty in its very simplicity.

Your days of chaos and conflict are drawing very quickly to an end and for some this is already the case.

Your Diamond Lights wait in much anticipation for your company and for your exploration. They have been placed within you by the Divine, for you are Divine and our only request is your Remembrance of the Truth, for it is the only Gateway to Love and Joy and Freedom of the Heart and Soul. You are deserving of this or you would not be in Hueman form. You will discover through a very simple and beautiful process, the Gifts and Challenges that your Soul has chosen for itself in the journey of Remembrance of your Divine Love and your Divine Light.

With Love from I, the Mother, I now invite you to explore and express All of who you are and are Infinitely Becoming.

PLANET, NUMBER & SYMBOL ASSOCIATED WITH EACH DIAMOND LIGHT

NEPTUNE & PLUTO	◇	10	CHALICE
URANUS	◇	9	STAR
SATURN	◇	8	DOLPHIN & WHALE
JUPITER	◇	7	CROWN
MARS	◇	6	SWORD
SUN	◇	5	DIAMOND
VENUS	◇	4	ROSE
MERCURY	◇	3	PEARL
MOON	◇	2	WATER

EARTH ◇ 1 STONE

THE UNION OF THE DIAMOND LIGHTS 'DARION'

We, the Union of Love and First Light, wish to remind you that we as you, are Multi-Dimensional Beings. We express from the One Grand Consciousness of Love and express this Love through Light. One of the most pure expressions of this Light is your Sun, and another is electrical current that is expressed through the power and the beauty of Lightning.

As we have said, the Tree of Life is a Holygram of your Universe and a Holygram of YOU.

The Holygram of the Universe is expressed through your planets and the elements within those planets, so this must mean that it is also the expression of your Diamond Lights and the elements of those Diamond Lights.

We wish now to express to you the very wonder, the very miracle of these Diamond Lights through a divine aspect of our consciousness which chooses to be called Darion.

It is with great love that I now reach into your minds and your hearts to assist you in the remembrance, the holiness of this Holygram that you find your Souls residing in.

Many of you are very open to universal perceptions and universal truths of exactly what this Tree of Life you find yourselves in is actually and truly about. For you to truly receive the gifts presented to you in these Diamond Lights, I wish to convey to you what I, Darion, through many experiences of expansion have come to know as Truth. A great sadness for us, the Union, is the incredible spread of disease among your huemanity, whether it be physical, mental or emotional. Many great achievements have been created, many great healers have inspired, many brave Souls have endured; however, none of these, in essence, has cured you completely, wholly and unconditionally.

For without the Foundation of Knowledge and Truth, which brings the awakening of Love, of Soul, all your methods will only take you to a certain point of purity, of wellness and of well-being.

It is time for you to realise that You are the Universe, as we have already expressed in these Scriptions, so I now take you on a journey into the holy realms of your minds, your bodies and your emotions, so that a door of Truth may be opened in each and everyone of these beautiful Gateways of Love and Light expressed therein.

I wish to begin with the Diamond Light of One, the Diamond Light that rests under your feet. For your 'hueman experience' this would have to be the most powerful and most potent for your optimum healing and health, for within it, symbolically and energetically, it contains the vibrations of your most powerful minerals and crystals. It is the Diamond Light where the love, the wisdom and the nurturing of your Earth enters. It is the Foundation of your Auric Fields. You must begin to see this Auric Field more as a 'Force Field of Light' that supports, nurtures and protects. As you have pondered for many lifetimes the question: 'which came first, the chicken or the egg?' In your hueman expression we wish to say, without the Egg, without the protective shell, the hueman form could

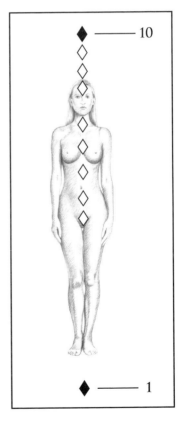

81

not survive.

So to answer that hueman question, it is the energy field, the Force Field of Light, the Shell, that you must firstly bring your attention to, for in essence you are all precious and beautiful beings encased in a Shell of Light, experiencing yourselves in an Infinite Ocean of Love.

So as many of you live without your feet on the Earth, your bodies become weak, your shell becomes soft, your Light Force becomes damaged. The concrete and metals you walk on cannot provide you with the crystalline minerals and elements that are required to keep this Force Field of Light, this Shell, strong and whole. Everything outside this Shell of Light can, and does, have some impact on it, so it is of utmost importance that it is kept clear, strong and vibrant. So for the purpose of the teaching we wish to take you, in this expression of Truth, onto the Infinite Symbol of Love. So as your attention now rests on the Diamond Light of ONE, we wish you to spiral your way to the top, to the Diamond Light of TEN. For understand, We the Union wish to bring Union to You, wish to bring Union to your Hueman Tree. So as has been said before, it is a Union of 'As Above, So Below'. It is a Union of balance, harmony, dark and light.

So as we now draw your attention to the Diamond Light of TEN, understand the relationships between this Diamond Light of TEN, the Unmanifest, the unknown, and this Diamond Light of ONE, your Earth, is a very important sacred relationship indeed, for ONE cannot Be without the Other. The Diamond Light of TEN, as we have expressed, is your Neptune and your Pluto. In astrological terms, each of your planets has a personality, has a will, has an essence, has a vibration. This, of course, is Truth. The Diamond Light of TEN is the Unmanifest, the Abyss, the Great Womb of the Mother, which is represented by the Zero and where All That Is has been birthed from, including YOU, and the ONE of the masculine, the ONE of first consciousness coming into manifestation. And to take the essence of this Diamond Light a step further, we know of your fear of those things outside and inside of yourselves that you may not understand or of which you may not be aware.

There has been much experience in your hueman condition of what you call negative energies, what you call psychic attacks and entities. Many of you in your spiritual practice have spent long hours and much energy trying to protect yourself from these energies or to repel these energies. You must now understand a Universal Truth, which when fully embraced will set you Free.

No-thing whether it be negative, positive, seen or unseen can go against your Free Will. God and Goddess and All That Is do not go against Your Will, so if you choose to hand your Will over to another, whether it be seen or unseen, that is a Choice you Make.

It is a choice that can debilitate and brings the energy of Victim into your Light Force, into this protective shell. Your own Free Wills are the very thing that can keep this Shell of Light pure, clear and energised.

So to assist you in this teaching we wish to make it very clear that 'As Above So Below'.

So if you allow these energies that you perceive as negative to enter your 'Force Field of Light' by lack of Will, they will enter through the Diamond Light of the TEN and be made manifest in the Diamond Light of the ONE, and as they enter the Diamond Light of the ONE, they will first express themselves in your Light Field, as what you may call anxiety, nervousness and fear, and within the blink of an eye, this energy can travel through your Light Field and enter into the Gateways of the other Diamond Lights; for, understand, this Force Field of Light, this Shell of Light must be entered into first before anything can enter into the Gateway of another Diamond Light. This may assist you in understanding the importance of your relationships with your Earth and with your Heaven.

Your Earth, as you are, is here to be of service. Your Mother and the purity and the innocence of her 'inner-child' wish to give to you all the healing and love that is required for you to experience All That You Are in the safety of this Shell of Pure Love and Pure Light.

Both the Diamond Light of the ONE and the Diamond Light of the TEN, the ONE ZERO, are very powerful magnetic Gateways and for the teachings of these Gateways we wish to keep simplicity as the utmost ideal.

They are the Gateways in which you first create then manifest every thought, feeling and experience in your hueman lives, and we wish you to know that in Truth both God and Goddess are the Gatekeepers of these two Diamond Lights. And once more for the simplicity of the teaching, in your meditation, in your quiet time, in your imagination, you may see God and Goddess as the Gatekeepers of these Diamond Lights and you may call on them and know that they are there for you to experience pure love and pure light once more.

I wish now to take you into the wonder and the beauty of the Diamond Light of TWO, which is expressed in the energy of your Tree as the MOON. Technically speaking, your Moon is not what you call a planet, it is a rock; however, spiritually speaking, do not be fooled by appearances. What appears to be a rock is a very powerful psychic ball of Light and Knowing. This, as you have been told, sits energetically at the base of your body, at the base of your spine. It is the psychic ball of cycles, of emotion, of illusion. As many years ago you were told of the truth of your bio-rhythms, the cycles in which your body rotates, so the Moon holds the bio-rhythms not only of your emotional bodies, not only of your Oceans, but also of your Diamond

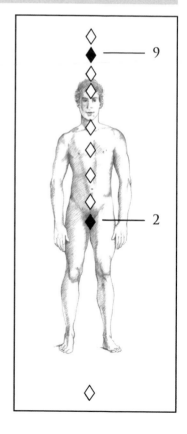

Light of NINE. For your NINE Diamond Light is your planet URANUS on your Tree of Life, and your planet Uranus in Kabbalistic teaching represents the planet of the First Light, so, understand, from the Unmanifest Pluto, first form appeared as Neptune and first expression of that form was Uranus, First Light. And for those of you whose wits aren't quite about them at present, understand that the Universe will speak to you in many languages and in many ways, some being a little more 'Base' than others. So as you look at the spelling of your planet Uranus, it is interesting to note where your Moon sits! This is what we call a teaching tool for your remembrance and assimilation.

So First Light sits in the Diamond Light of NINE and is reflected with the light of the Moon and her cycles, her bio-rhythms and of course as you are all aware, the fertility cycle of the female form is a reflection of your Moon cycles, for it represents the female aspect and is so reflected back in the holygram of your bodies.

Your Diamond Light of TWO regulates the cycles of your bodies (which can also be expressed as your tides and seasons). In a 24-hour day you essentially have three hueman cycles of the Eight, which, when followed, will assist in the strengthening of your hueman well-being. There is the Eight Cycle of sleep, the Eight Cycle of work, and the Eight Cycle of play and reflection.

Your Diamond Light of NINE represents the Spiritual Cycles of your Soul, your Souls rest, your Soul's work, and your Soul's play and reflection. It is the highest aspect of your Soul; it is the First Light, the First Starburst of your Consciousness from the Great Womb of the Mother, and as the Great Womb of the Mother rests above you, so she rests within you; so, understand, by allowing Union of the Diamond Light of the TWO and the Diamond Light of the NINE you can allow for the hueman experience of Heaven on Earth.

This TWO Diamond Light, this energy of the Moon that governs your Oceans also is the master of your own inner ocean. It magnetically and energetically influences the fluids and their cycles within your bodies.

The Second Diamond Light directly influences your kidneys, your bladder and the adrenal glands that rest on your kidneys. So for the purpose of purity, of well-being that we are expressing here, we ask that if anybody is experiencing afflictions within their renal systems, that they bathe in moonlight and lovingly create 'moon water' to drink; that they bathe in the oceans, asking for healing to take place and asking for fears to be dissolved, and asking for Light, the Light of the Mother, to be placed in this second Diamond Light. For, understand, the dark cycles of the Moon represent your unconscious and your fears, and the Light cycles of the Moon represent your illumination, the Truth of your Higher Self in the NINE Diamond Light.

And for those of you experiencing anxiety, tiredness or exhaustion, we ask that you sit on your Mother Earth bringing the Diamond Light of TWO in Union with the Diamond Light of the ONE and request that the Diamond Light of the ONE be filled with the richness and the Love of the Earth and the Light of the Moon bringing strength and renewed vitality to your Shells of Light.

We now in the teaching move on to the Diamond Light of THREE, the Diamond Light of your creativity, your naivety and your sexuality. This, as you are probably beginning to realise, is in direct Union with your Diamond Light of EIGHT at the Crown of your head. This is a most auspicious Union indeed for your Diamond Light of EIGHT, as in the Kabbalistic teaching, is the Diamond Light of the First Form of First Physical Being, so it is interesting to note that it rests on the top of your physical being.

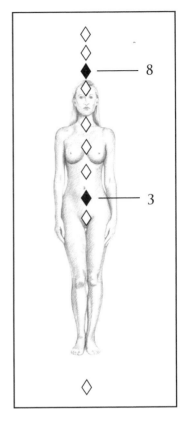

EIGHT as you have been repeatedly told, is your Infinite Symbol of Love and Light. It is first creation and manifestation of your hueman bodies, so, of course, Union with your THREE Diamond Light, where you in your hueman form create and manifest other hueman beings, again is a very powerful Union indeed.

This third Diamond Light, if you choose to perceive it this way, is in the triad of the Moon and the Goddess, and your EIGHT Diamond is in the triad of the Stars, but is still represented by the Mother.

Your emotional bodies manifest themselves, not completely, but very powerfully and potently, within this Diamond Light of THREE. Utmost importance must be given to the strengthening and the purification of this Diamond Light, for it can be very easily bogged down with repressed emotions, confusion and dissolution. It is your hueman centre of creativity of expression of your physical bodies through your sexuality and, as we have said, your naivety. For it is here where your inner-child rests within your bodies and where the innocence and the purity of you is remembered and stored.

So to contaminate this centre with impure or blocked emotions will and does affect the overall well-being of your happiness, of your joy, of your truth, of your innocence and the truth of your purity.

So by bringing your awareness to the Crown, to the EIGHT, to the purity of the First Form as the purity of a child that grows in this third region of the female body, to bring back the awareness into the Diamond Light of EIGHT of your innocence, of your purity, of your form of the child within, this shall create a very harmonious, open and loving experience in all your relationships.

Again for simplicity of the teaching, the ways and means in which you can purify the third Diamond Light, is once more bathe in your oceans and streams and to also communicate with the creatures of your sea, your dolphins, your whales. For, understand, that the experience had by many a hueman being when in communication with your dolphins and your whales, is that of pure joy, of pure innocence, of pure play, like that of an infant. To commune with these creatures will bring remembrance of your own purity, your own joy and your own playfulness back to the Diamond Light of THREE.

You may also wish again to use the vibration of your moon and stars by allowing yourself to bathe in their light and to ask that the light of the moon and the stars be concentrated in the Diamond Light of THREE and the Diamond Light of EIGHT, to purify your memories back to the innocence of a child and to initiate new emotional beginnings free of pain and fear.

The Union of these Diamond Lights of THREE and EIGHT will be profound indeed to all your emotional experience and relationships with your self and others, and when in harmony, will bring joy and peace, laughter and play, back into lives that have not experienced this for many of their evolutions.

As we leave the triad of the Moon, we now approach with deep reverence and respect the Diamond Light of your FOUR.

This is the Gateway through which your Soul projects its essence, for the Soul itself does not live in your physical body, but projects itself through the Gateway of this Diamond Light of FOUR into the physical body. It is the point of power for your Soul, for it plugs itself into your being so it may relay electrically, emotionally and physically its messages and guidance. This very powerful point in your bodies, this Diamond Light of FOUR, amplifies your Soul's yearning, your Soul's knowledge, and often your Soul's despair. It is a point of much physical purification, for it takes in the regions of your LIVER and your STOMACH, and this is where you process your physical nourishment; however, it is also where you process your Soul's journey, your Soul's instruction and intentions.

Much care must be taken not to allow a certain aspect of the SEVEN Diamond Light called the EGO, to take control or override the Diamond Light of the FOUR.

If the Ego overrides the Higher Mind, it is because the Ego is experiencing doubt and an over-expression of Ego, which will find its way into the Solar Plexus and will create the energy of doubt there also. For when you focus only on your individuality and not the higher aspect of your Soul, you will only bring doubt into your worthiness, into your Soul's purpose, for understand this: the Soul is powerful but your Soul is also vulnerable, for it is still experiencing many aspects of itself; it is constantly discovering; it is a pioneer, therefore it finds itself in unknown territories.

So the Ego, the 'I am', will come along

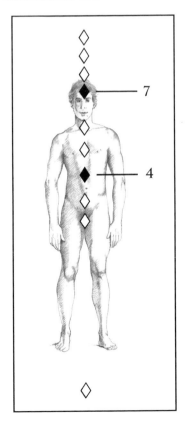

and appear to rescue the Soul when the Soul is feeling lost and vulnerable in its hueman experience; so, rest assured, the Ego will lead the Soul astray if the Ego is allowed to take control of the journey.

Much could be taught about these two Diamond Lights of FOUR and SEVEN, and shall be in later teachings, for the battle of Union between the Soul and the Ego has been a very potent and powerful battle indeed in your hueman experience, but do rest assured Union of Ego and Soul 'WILL BE'.

So it is important to remain in the higher aspect of your SEVEN, of your Jupiter, which is the expansion of your Higher Mind, and allow that expansion of the Higher Mind to gently filter its way down into your Soul's sacred light, so your Soul may have the highest guidance and the highest knowledge and wisdom at all times. For, understand too, the fear of LIVING that many of you experience will reside in your LIVE-R, and that fear, if fuelled by your Ego, will create ANGER; for your Ego fears that if it follows your Soul unconditionally and gives it all its trust, it will be in D-ANGER.

So understand that your Liver can hold the energy of your Ego's experience of anger, for it fears the danger of losing its very identity. This very experience is the only thing stopping you from experiencing the Sacred Chambers of your Hearts, for when you find yourself Being in your Heart, you realise you are All One; you realise you are free of identity, free of hueman illusion, that you are All One Heart, beating One Song. And your Ego fears it will be cast aside, that it will be destroyed, but this is not so. Your Ego will be relieved that it does not have to perform, that it does not have to feel *anger* at being put in *danger* of extinction.

Your Ego, your identity, will be made glorious and shall realise its Divinity as a unique expression. Your Ego has just forgotten it is Divine so it does battle with your Soul, a relentless task master that puts it under pressure to remember its true identity of Love and Light.

You all have within you the Divine Mind, perfect sight and a consciousness of great beauty and truth. Allow that to support, to nurture and guide your Soul's sacred journey on the Infinite Symbol of Eternal Love and Eternal Light. For you see, there is nowhere else to travel, so do not hold up your journey, in doubt and anger, for it is only the doubt and anger that holds you back in expressing your Soul's Highest Manifestation of itself while in your Earthly experience, and that saddens us and we know it saddens you very deeply.

So be brave enough to be happy and show through your hueman expression, what Joy the Union of the Diamond Lights of FOUR and SEVEN will bring.

To assist you in this great challenge of Union of your Diamond Light of FOUR and your Diamond Light of SEVEN, we wish to suggest that you go stand in your Sunshine, and ask your Sun, which is the manifestation of what you may call your Christ Consciousness, ask for the Rays of the Sun to fill your Diamond Lights of your SEVEN and your FOUR. Ask the Light of your Sun to embrace your Soul and your Ego, to nourish and to strengthen them, to bring the Divine Love and to shine the Divine Light of the Sun into these Diamond Lights. See each Diamond Light become a radiant Golden Ball and allow the Infinite Symbol of Love and Light to begin to spiral between these two Golden Diamond Lights. This will truly and positively assist in the process before each and every one of you.

As we travel to the very Heart of this Central Triad, the Triad of your Soul and Sun, we feel and know great joy, great love, and great pleasure, for as we now enter and experience the Sacred Chambers of your Heart, we are awe-struck by this Diamond Light of FIVE.

As you in your hueman experience have many challenges, so do we, the Union, have ours. Our challenge in these Scriptions, is now to express exactly what this Diamond Light of FIVE is to you, in hueman terms.

For it contains within it, power of Love, and power of Light that transcends all description, all knowledge, all conceptions, all dreams and all desires. We cannot 'speak' the language of the Heart, but we honour you in your songs, in your poems and your plays at attempting to express and interpret the language of your Heart.

And as your Sun in your Solar System brings life and warmth and growth to you and your planet, so the Sun in your Hueman Being Universe is the source of your life and your growth. This Central Flame of Love is burning with desire for expression. The symbol of the Diamond, which has been placed in the Diamond Light of FIVE, is still in all its beauty and its awe, an inadequate representation of this centre, of this Flame, of all life, be it within you, be it around you or be it beyond all that you know. For it is the Light Force of the Source. It is the desire and the love of the Source, of All That Is, whether it be in your Universe, other Universes or Star Systems beyond your hueman comprehension.

For as we have said, the language of your Heart in true essence, cannot be expressed, for as the Diamond that resides there is pure

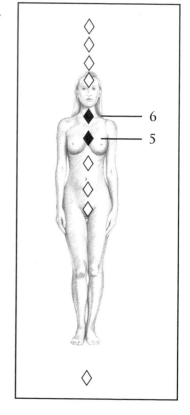

and clear, any 'interpretation' of the language of your Heart is one of some distortion. However, your Diamond Light of SIX is a vehicle for your hueman experience; it allows through desire and intention the expression in some form of what is inexpressible in its purity.

Your Diamond Light of SIX is, in its purity and its essence, the vehicle of communication for the language of your Heart. This Diamond Light of SIX however, also serves the purpose of communicating the language of your mind, the language of your emotions, the language of your fears, the language of your doubts and the language of your desires. This Gateway of SIX is there, in its purity, to communicate the Divine Will of your Heart and your Soul; however, more often than not it is used to communicate your Hueman Will, or what you call the Free Will of your mind. This too is important; however, for this teaching, which is in essence to assist you in your evolution, we must ask you to shift a gear, to release your Free Will to communication of the Divine Will. This is the pure purpose of the Diamond Light of SIX, and we do understand the journey, that it is and was important to you to express Free Will. But Free Will in its essence is the vehicle that leads you to the destination of Divine Will.

It is time to surrender to your Hearts, for up to this point, which in Truth has served a very Divine purpose, you have surrendered to your Free Wills, to your Egos, to your doubts, to your fears, and make no mistake, the force of energy that's released from the Diamond Light of SIX is very powerful indeed, whether it be an expression of your Free Will or your Divine Will, it does resonate and finds its way into your Auric Field and into the world in which you live.

This Diamond Light of SIX has been given the Symbol of the Sword, and we are asking you now to put down your Swords, to surrender to the Divine Will within, to the Will of God/Goddess/All That Is, for when you do this your Heart will open in Joy and Love and the Divine Connection shall be re-established and the Flame of your Hearts shall burn with a Light and a Love beyond your words and ours.

> *To assist you in this process of surrender and transformation, we wish you, through your mind's eye, to see and feel a beautiful flame burning within the Sacred Chamber of your FIVE Diamond Light, and as this flame burns deep within your Hearts, see the flame begin to dance and spiral and rise up to the Sword in your throat. See this Sword melt in the heat of the flame; see the Sword become a beautiful pure flow of silver and see that silver gently release itself back into the flame bringing greater Light and Strength to the Flame, bringing Union of the Diamond Light of the SIX with the Diamond Light of the FIVE.*

So the energy expressed through the Diamond Light of the SIX is fuelled with the Love and the Purity of your Hearts; for, make no mistake, when you speak from your Heart, you speak the Truth, and the Truth is your only protection while experiencing the often vulnerable times in your hueman experience.

Understand, when Union comes for the Diamond Light of the FIVE and the Diamond Light of the SIX, they become the UNI-VERSE. The Uni, the One, the Diamond Light of your Hearts will express itself through VERSE, the Diamond Light of your VOICE. This is Truth, and put another way: Let One Voice Exist - The Voice of your Heart.

LET
ONE
VOICE
EXIST

THE VOICE
OF
YOUR HEART

THE MAGIC OF ELEVEN

As you may or may not realise, we, the Union of Love and Light, through the teachings of these Scriptions, are wishing to express to you a simple but very important formula of your very being, of your very existence.

We have spoken of each of the Diamond Lights through various aspects of our consciousness and all of these Scriptions have brought different aspects of your Diamond Lights to your awareness. In these Scriptions we have also shown the Union between these Diamond Lights. If you observe a little closer, you will see that the Union of these Diamond Lights, whether it be your 1 and your 10, your 2 and your 9, your 3 and your 8, your 4 and your 7, or your 5 and your 6, their Union brings them to Eleven (11).

Again we shall 'play' on your words as this brings us much Joy, and you much Truth; for, understand, that Joy can only come from Truth.

Your Eleven, your double one, can and does mean many things, however, to break down your word EL-EVEN, we would like to express the 'EL' is what we call an abbreviation of the word 'ELOHIM' the name of GOD, and your EVEN is an expression of your Equality. You are a reflection, a direct manifestation, a perfect mirror-image of GOD, of the 'ELOHIM', which is also described as the Angelic Beings who represent the Divine Order of God/Goddess/All That Is.

So with the conscious Union of your Diamond Lights you also become the conscious Union of God/Goddess/All That Is. All That Is You, Infinitely. The magic number of Eleven is your Key to THE ONE you have always been.

You are ONE with the Source, you are ONE with the Universe, we ask you now to be ONE with your HEARTS and with your SOULS, for this is the journey and the destination.

In your Kabbalistic system of numerology:

$$E = 5$$

$$L = 3$$

$$\text{'EL'} = 8$$

$$E = 5$$

$$V = 6$$

$$E = 5$$

$$N = 5$$

$$\text{'EVEN'} = 21(3)$$

So 'EL' (8) and 'EVEN' (3) add up to 11.

* The 'el' or 'al' ending of many of the Angelic names is a reference to GOD, and when used on its own, means just that.

UNION WITH CREATION 'DARION'

I, Darion, once more bring you greetings of eternal Love, eternal Light and, willingly, eternal laughter.

Each and every Heart, each and every Soul, and each and every Mind is now receiving Purification, receiving Light and receiving Love. For only Love and Light can bring the Purification that is required now by your Mind, your Heart and Your Soul, at this point in your Evolution.

There are many ways to enhance, promote and guide the purification process; however, nothing other than Love, and the Light produced by that Love, can bring the purification required and yearned for by every Heart, every Soul and every Mind. There are many tools, many formulas and many belief systems that all lead you on the road to purification, that will show you the way, that will give you the map, but on the journey it is only the purification that can bring the initiation and then the pure transformation back into the One Heart, the One Soul, the One Union with Love and Light.

So, understand, each of you on this Infinite spiral of Love and Light is an 'essence' travelling the path back to purity of Spirit, purity of Heart. Many Souls for many lifetimes have taken the Tools, have followed the Maps, but as they draw close to the Pool, the Destination of Purification, they realise they have to let go of the Tools and the Maps that brought them here, back to the 'ONE'.

So, through many lifetimes, attachments are formed to these Tools and to these Maps, and understand that these Tools and these Maps can come in many forms. The most predominant of these Tools is your relationships with others, for it is through the experience and exploration of another's Heart and another's Soul that we find comfort and conflict on the path back to the One Pure Essence, the ONE PURE SPIRIT.

We understand your dilemma in putting down your Tools and your Maps, your Maps being your belief systems, the way you think you should arrive at your destination. Your Maps are also your attitudes, your past experiences and your present perceptions. Some Maps have brought a positive direction and others have had you going around in circles many times over!

The Source has allowed its Divine Souls, its Divine Aspects, to travel along the Infinite Braid of Love and Light, always being of assistance through these Tools and Maps; however, the Source now wishes to carry you back HOME without any effort on your part. The Pool of Purity, the Great River of Life, the Rainbow Serpent wishes to embrace you, wishes to bring you back into the ONE HEART, the ONE MIND, and the ONE SOUL. It does not mean that you shall disappear into a puff of smoke; it does not mean that existence as you know it, or your hueman experience, will come to an end. What it does mean is the experience and exploration of Heaven on Earth, here and now, in this time and in this space.

Each and every Heart, Mind and Soul has been given a Divine Gift, has been given purity, love and light, so that it may be made manifest through you, as you - so that Heaven may be experienced in the Hueman Heart.

Our Scriptions have attached to them some urgency, some concern, for the magnitude of this Union with the One Source, God/Goddess/All That Is, is of the greatest importance, not just to you, your loved ones and your Universe, but to us, the Union of Love, the Union of Light; for we, like you, are on a path of expansion and evolution.

We, as you, have had our own crossroads, our own challenges; for remember, 'As Above So Below'.

So we understand your position, we understand your apprehension, we understand the great change that is now taking place within you and around you.

But we must amplify the importance of you embracing these Scriptions, for to deny your Truth, your Divinity and your Union with all Creation, shall only bring more heartache, more illusion, more disease of which none of you deserve, or for that matter have ever deserved.

We now set before you a new sort of Map, a new Tool, another dimension to these Diamond Lights which your hueman condition shall understand with ease, with grace and with curiosity.

The gifts and challenges specific to each Diamond Light have been put in the simplest and purest Scriptions for the benefit of course of the teachings.

Within each of the Scriptions of these Diamond Lights which we now place before you, there is Infinite Knowledge and Eternal Truths. Much shall be written in future Scriptions about these Diamond Lights; however, we wish you to concentrate on this Map set before you, to understand the journey in which you all, with your Divine Wills, have given permission to experience.

These Maps shall show you where you are, what your Soul is aspiring to, what your 'Gift' from the Source is, and the challenges associated with those gifts in your hueman experience.

For if there were no challenge, you would not appreciate the gift. As, if there was no Dark, you could not admire the beauty of the Light that radiates from the stars in the sky at night.

So understand the Challenge as the very Foundation of Creation, for the gifts that wish to shine through you and for you, and for all those you love and for all those you don't.

We trust and know that the following teaching will bring comfort, excitement, support and truth and it is our greatest joy to bring this to you now, for you are our brothers and our sisters. You are all Truth, you are all Love and you are all Light. Please remember this Now, not just for you but for your children and your children's children. And to give of yourself the gifts that are Divine and True, is the greatest gift any Being in any Universe can give.

THE SACRED EQUATION

It is now that we ask you to receive the Sacred Formula of your Souls. The equation for Knowledge, Truth and the experience of Love are all within your date of Earth Birth. Understand that the Love of the Mother and the Truth of the Father are the creators of the Child Knowledge.

As you have already been told, you are all Father, Mother and Child. The Sacred numerals of your birth date are your key to that Love, that Truth and that Knowledge.

As we have previously expressed, all the teachings of your numerals to this point are true and correct, and also as we have expressed, everything is in the process of expansion so new ideas, new equations and new expressions are being birthed here and now, in your space and time.

We wish to divide this Sacred Equation of your Earth Birth into Three Aspects and these three aspects will show you the Holy Trinity that lies within each and every Hueman Being.

Each aspect of this Holy Trinity is, in essence, a Spiritual Temple of Light and these Temples of Light exist in the Three Triads of Diamond Lights within your bodies. These three Temples of Light are also represented by the Central Pillar of your Tree of Life.

THE THREE TEMPLES OF THE DIAMOND LIGHT SYSTEM

10

9

TEMPLE OF THE STARS

8

7

STARS
FIRST LIGHT
KNOWLEDGE

6

5

TEMPLE OF THE SUN

4

SUN
CENTRAL FLAME
TRUTH

3

2

TEMPLE OF THE MOON

1

MOON
DIVINE REFLECTION
LOVE

THREE TEMPLES
OF LIGHT: THE STARS,
THE SUN & THE MOON

Each Temple of Light represents the DAY, MONTH or YEAR of your Earth Birth.

THE DAY YOU ARE BORN resonates within your Temple of Starlight where all aspects of the Soul's mind and memory are created and put into thought-form by the Soul. So your DAY numeral represents the MIND and the individual identity or ego the Soul has chosen for a life cycle, so it may experience KNOWLEDGE.

THE MONTH YOU ARE BORN resonates in your Temple of Sunlight, where all aspects of the Soul's heart and desires are put into emotional form by the Soul. So the MONTH numeral represents the HEART and the individual expression the Soul has chosen for a life cycle so it may experience TRUTH.

THE YEAR YOU ARE BORN (not the century) resonates in your Temple of Moonlight where all aspects of the Soul's reflection and cycles are created and put into action by the Soul. So your YEAR numeral represents the SOUL and the individual purpose the Soul has chosen for a life cycle so it may experience LOVE.

We wish to express that in the YEAR you were born, that you only use the last two digits of your birthday; for, understand, the CENTURY in which you are born is the 'playing field', if you choose, that your Soul has wished to come in on to express itself.

THE CENTURY OF UNION

The CENTURY in which you are born is the energetic vibration the Earth and the Souls upon her wish to endure and wish to expand upon as a GROUP SOUL.

So, understand, to take this a step further, your 20th Century, your 1900s, is the vibration in which all of you in communion with these Scriptions have birthed yourselves. It was a century of discovery between the Self and the Universe, with the One being the Self, the Nine being the Universe.

You travelled long and hard in those one hundred years, discovering more about the Self, but also the world around you and the Universe in which you live. You created satellites, and you are sending shuttles to spaces never before dreamt of by man. And in that expansion and that expression of wishing to experience your Universe in your last quarter of that century, you also with intensity, went within, through your self exploration, through your workshops and through your self-inquiry.

It was a century of extremes. It was a century of exploration. It was a century of enormous freedom and enormous restriction. All Souls that earthed themselves in that playing field of the 20th century came for dynamic expansion of one form or another. And, understand, your 1900's, the One and the Nine when in Union (added together) come back to the ONE, come back to the Self. This has been a very important part of the Soul's journey; however, now the Soul is being asked to leap into Union with your '2000'. For, understand, two is partnership, two is Union, and, as we have shown you, Two is the Goddess.

You are now in the middle of a great tidal change, a wave of huge proportions. You cannot resist this Wave or this Waterfall Way. So the 'playing field' has changed and the 'ground rules', if you choose, are also in the process of changing. You are now here for the Soul to experience Union. You are the Holy Trinity, you are the Mother, the Father and the Child. You are the Mind, the Heart and the Soul of the One Source. So the DAY you are born will reflect the gifts and challenges of your MIND. The MONTH you are born will reflect the gifts and challenges of your HEART, and the YEAR of the Century you are born in will reflect the gifts and challenges of your SOUL.

To simplify this even further, as we set before you the gifts and the challenges of each sacred number of your Earth Birth, we wish to give the gift and the challenge of the Heart and Soul in two ways. An example would be: if the Month number you were born was a three, the month of March, you would refer to the Three Gift Vibration as guidance for your HEART or the emotional gift and challenge of this life cycle.

And if the YEAR you were born was a Five, you would refer to the Five Gift Vibration for the gift and challenge of your Soul's chosen purpose.

However, as we have said: all is coming back into Union; your Heart and Soul are coming back into Union. So, if you choose, you could add the Three Heart and the Five Soul to bring it into what we would like to express as an Eight Union or HOUL Vibration.

Again, with purpose and passion we 'play' with your words. Union of the Heart with the Soul brings your Spiritual expression into Hueman Houliness, or the Heart Of Unconditional Love.

HEART
OF
UNCONDITIONAL
LOVE

So, you may approach this Sacred equation in two ways, for, understand, each of you are All these gifts and All these challenges, no matter what your Earth Birth numerals. We are just putting before you the individual expressions which your Mind, your Heart and your Soul have come to experience.

The information, however, in all the gift vibrations will also bring much knowledge to each individual.

The DAY you are born, the Soul's Mind expression, we wish to keep in extreme simplicity. For the benefit of the mind we have put before you a simple chart stating the gift and the challenge.

This diagram also associates with the Heart and Soul vibrations, and we have given detailed information about these because they relate to the very Heart and Soul of the teaching.

The mind only needs one word to then create a thousand words, a thousand thoughts and a thousand visions.

So we do not wish to hinder the experience of the Heart and the Soul with the complexities of the Mind; for your mind will still have to digest and clarify the information given in relation to the Heart and the Soul. So the mind's gift and challenge are being expressed in the utmost simplicity.

You may wish to also use your traditional numerology to play with and explore the information set before you now, for you shall still find truth and knowledge with any formula you choose to use.

Remember, you are the Divine Creators and we are only putting before you the tools and the material to create whatever you choose yourselves to be.

This information of your Sacred Equation is for the Divine purpose of Love and Truth and Knowledge, for just as your Souls have been birthed from Love and Truth, understand, you are the child of Knowledge, and all that Knowledge, Love and Truth may be remembered through the Sacred Numbers of your Earth Birth.

A SACRED
EQUATION EXAMPLE

We wish to share with you a more detailed example of a Sacred Equation and our 'channel' has kindly offered her 'Earth Birth' for this process. In love and laughter we kindly thank Starlight's Ego for allowing us to disclose such information.

The Sacred Equation for 23 June 1958 is:

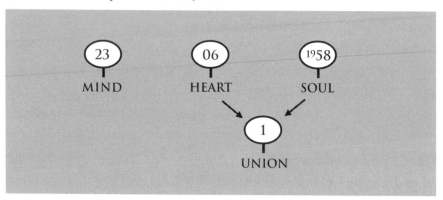

You always add the numbers until you arrive at a single digit. This also applies to what you traditionally call your Master numbers or double symbol numerals; e.g. 11, 22, 33 etc.

It does mean however that the intensity of the single digit would be amplified in the Soul's experience of the gift and challenge. A "10" symbol would reduce back to the One, (as zero is the un-manifest).

So Starlight arrived at her Earth Birth with a:

FIVE MIND VIBRATION	SIX HEART VIBRATION
FOUR SOUL VIBRATION	ONE UNION VIBRATION

THE FIVE MIND VIBRATION gives Starlight the gift to transform information for others - hence her channelling abilities, but alas her challenge is the need for constant confirmation mentally of the information she receives, whether it be from us, the Union, or her fellow hueman beings. So the receiving of these Scriptions has given her and us the opportunity to enhance her gift and transform her challenge.

THE SIX HEART VIBRATION gives Starlight the gift to express the truth to others and to express information for Spirit; however, her challenge has been to emotionally surrender, not resist her own Divine Will, and be able to speak her own truth. So, through surrender, her Heart is then allowed to experience being of Service, which in return gives her emotional nourishment and security.

THE FOUR SOUL VIBRATION gives Starlight the gift to inspire others to get in touch with their own Soul's Journey and respond to their abilities (hence these Scriptions!); however, the challenge for her is to nurture and support herself, and not fall into the trap of self-criticism, for to allow the passion and purpose of her Soul to be expressed will bring her the inner love and acceptance desired by all Souls.

THE ONE UNION VIBRATION would allow the highest purpose of Starlight's Heart and Soul to be expressed, which is the grounding of heaven on earth. And in Love and Truth, long before these Scriptions were received by her, we could feel her longing to be given exactly that, the experience of Heaven on Earth.

With the Union Vibration, no challenge exists in the experience, as your Heart and Soul are in Union and expressing fully their highest purpose.

Each and every Heart and Soul is now on the journey to that very Union, and each and every Union will see the Heart and Soul return to the full experience and expression of its 'Houliness'.

THE HUEMAN PATH OF UNION

SPIRITUAL GIFT	DIAMOND LIGHT	HUEMAN CHALLENGE
THE UNMANIFEST	10	CREATION
OBSERVATION	9	CONTAMINATION
INTEGRATION	8	CONDEMNATION
REALIZATION	7	ILLUSION
SURRENDER	6	RESISTANCE
TRANSFORMATION	5	CONFIRMATION
RESPONSIBILITY	4	PERSECUTION
INITIATION	3	CONFUSION
FOUNDATION	2	DESTRUCTION
UNIFICATION	1	SEPARATION

THE PATH OF SERVICE

The gifts and the challenges set before you are your growth, are your way, are your Map, back to the One Heart, the One Mind, and the Love of ONE. Your Soul and its association with your Free Will has chosen whether to access these gifts or not in previous lifetimes. The time has come however, for each and every Soul to resonate and vibrate with the Gifts given to them by the Love of One, for this is the way of your evolution as an individual Soul and as the Group Soul of Huemanity. We cannot hold back our intention and our teaching from you any longer as it is a very important part of the Grand Plan, the Grand Union that is taking place within you and around you.

Trust us when we say, no Soul can evolve further until they have accessed their gifts. For, understand, misinformation has been given to you about your Spirituality. Your Spirituality does not involve being 'psychic' or being greater or better than another. Being Spiritual does not even mean being in communication or relationship with your Guides and your Angels or even the One. The true essence and meaning of a Spiritual path is that of Being of Service to one another.

Many on their so-called Spiritual path have forgotten this. We do understand your need for inner discovery and we wish to support that and enhance that in any way we can. However, along the way of inner discovery many get lost in their own minds, their own feelings, their own problems and their own desires for growth, for change and for Truth.

We do not wish to dismay you in searching for your Truth, but the real Truth is, that by being of service with the gifts you have been given, of helping, nurturing, supporting and guiding others in your unique and special way - this is the True path of your Spirituality and only by doing and achieving this service can you find and embrace and Know the Love and Truth of the One. For, understand, the One has always been of Service to You.

I, the Mother, have sent many to represent Me on your Earth and of these essences, or energies if you choose, the one you would have called your ISIS, was sent with My energy to many civilisations and she was given many names. However, I wish to use the analogy of the Goddess ISIS to show you what I mean.

You may begin the action of Service by Surrendering to your Gift - not battling with it, not trying to change it, but accepting it and giving it permission to bring itself into full consciousness within you and for you. For to allow the Ego to step in and create your Gift in such a way that suits your idea of who you think you are, will only bring distress, confusion and conflict.

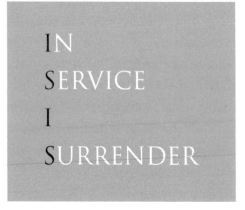

So, you can surrender to the Gift or you can surrender to the One and discover your Gift through the Will of God/Goddess/All That Is.

We are keeping the Gifts and Challenges now very simple and straight forward, for once the foundation of the Gift has been discovered and once you surrender to the Union of yourself with your Gift, it is then that you may decide which direction you wish to take with your Gift; how you wish to express it and how you wish to deal with and understand the challenge of that Gift, the challenge of your consciousness, the challenge of your Surrender and the challenge of being of Service. For many have been programmed to first be of Service to themselves before that of another. This is true in part; however, as we have said, it is very easy to lose yourself in your own belief systems and your own illusions and your own blockages, but through being of Service to another it is an easy, loving and effective way to clear your illusions, to clear your programming, to clear your blockages, for to Serve is to Give and to Give is a Gift. As Universal Law states: when you give you do receive with no effort required by you, for in the joy of giving you can only receive joy in return.

We, the Union, wish to bring forward to you a Being of Light by the name of ASHA, who has the ability to teach and entrust you now with this Knowledge.

I am Asha and I come to you from a place not known or even understood in your Time and Space. However, I can assure you that I travel to you through many stars, many galaxies and many Universes to be here with you now, and it is my greatest joy, my greatest pleasure and greatest desire to embrace each and every beautiful Heart and Soul, to bring them into Union, to bring them into Peace, to bring them into the Light and the Love that they already are. And to magnify that Love and that Light into a glorious, glorious Starburst of purity, of joy, of release and of Truth.
Each gift of the Diamond Lights shall now be given my full attention.

THE TRIAD
OF THE MOON

ONE GIFT VIBRATION

I wish to start from the ground up, so we shall begin with your Diamond Light of One. For those of you who vibrate to this number One, you may not have had many incarnations on the planet Earth before, and this would bring you automatically a feeling of separation, of loneliness, of doubt and fear; for, as has been explained in previous Scriptions, the Union of you as a One vibration with the Ten Vibration is of utmost importance for you to feel whole and for you to feel Union with yourself and with others.

Your first purpose is to be in Union with your Heart and your Soul. Your physical Earth rules this Diamond Light of One. Your Gift as a One vibration is your Union actually with your Earth, for bringing down through the Diamond Light of Ten the energy of the ONE, the energy of God/Goddess/All That Is, you become a natural, clear and open channel for the connection of Heaven and Earth; this is your Gift, and a great Gift it is indeed.

However, a One vibration must remember they are On the Earth, but not part of the Earth. You are an Angel of Light that gives the Gift of Heaven to Earth. Your challenge is not to feel alone; your challenge is to share yourself with the other beings on your planet. This may feel difficult to do, for your connection with the Diamond Light of Ten could give the impression of being disconnected in the eyes of others. In some respects you could feel misunderstood; you could feel alone and not be able to communicate. Your challenge is to be here, very much grounded on your EARTH, so you can be a natural conduit of Love and Light of Heaven, here on Earth.

> *To assist you with your challenge of feeling separate, disconnected and alone, we ask that you commune with Nature, commune with Animals, meditate with Crystals, commune with the Fairy Kingdom and the Elementals, and if your intention to connect with them is pure they will all bring a feeling of "Oneness" to you through their own connection to the Divine.*
>
> *Trust your Earth; Trust your Heaven, Trust your Heart and your Soul, for only then can you Trust another. And when you Trust another, as you Trust yourselves, you will have Union in your life, you will have Union with your Brothers and your Sisters.*

Your Gift is what keeps your planet 'Pulsing'. Your Gift is what keeps your planet providing for you and all others whether they be animal, mineral, vegetable or Ego. And when you learn to access your Gift you will be able to create sacred spaces of pure Love and pure Light; you will be able to feed and nourish your Mother Earth with your love and light and the love and light of Heaven, which are one and the same. You will feel companionship, support and nourishment from the Earth and from all beings that live on your Earth.

Your earth is in the process of expanding her consciousness and needs all the love and support and nurturing you can give to her, for assisting in raising her consciousness you will also assist yourself. As the One vibration you are a direct link between Heaven and Earth, and, yes, you are on the Earth but not of the Earth. Once you accept this, your challenge will dissolve and you will be free to give and receive abundantly and joyously.

TWO GIFT VIBRATION

The Diamond Light of Two is in vibrational Union with your Moon and the Moon amplifies the consciousness of your Soul. As has been written in these Scriptions, your moon reflects the light of your SUN, which is the vibration of your Soul. So the Moon, representing the consciousness of your Soul, lays down the foundation that your Soul requires on its path in each life-cycle.

However, like the Moon, your Earthly Foundations in which your Soul experiences itself, are Cyclic. Foundations have been taught to be permanent, to be unchangeable, to be rock solid, to be predictable, to be a guarantee of some kind; however, you must remember your foundations are cyclic like your Moon, like your seasons, like your bodies.

To resist your cycles of change in your daily lives, in your life's path, does bring much despair and can bring much destruction.

For to resist the natural cycles of your foundations can only bring destruction of them, for they are not being allowed to grow, create and move on. An example of this, to put it another way, would be you buying a home, you move into that home, you put furniture in that home, you put your creations in that home, you may paint that home, you may expand or detract from it. That home will have a natural cycle in your life. Many of you understand this, of being quite happy in a home and then something inside you says 'I must move'. Your internal world needs a different foundation, a different place to express itself, a different vibration. Many resist the change and will find, eventually, outside forces step in to make you move, to make you change. This principle applies to your homes, your relationships, your jobs and your belief systems.

You would have experienced previous life cycles in some form of confinement or institution such as a prison, monastery, or even worked long hours in a confined space, such as a mine shaft, and could even suffer from some form of claustrophobia in the present life cycle.

True foundations need to be seen as cyclic with a clear purpose running through them. The challenge, of course, is not to resist, and not try to destroy the great cycles of your Soul.

If you are a Two vibration, your Gift is in the expression of your actions and willingness to flow, to change and to be open to receiving and living these foundations, these true foundations that are required by your Soul and your Heart. To be adaptable, to flow freely, is the greatest foundation you can give yourself and others.

Your Gift is to BE this through your Actions, show others the joy and trust of flowing and ebbing in the great Ocean of Huemanity and allowing the great cycles within you to be free to express themselves. The challenge, of course, is not trying to destroy, control or change through Free Will and Ego, the natural progression and cycles of your foundations.

To be aware of when you are in 'destruction mode' shall we say, you could experience much back pain and digestive blockages, for trying to 'hold on' to what you think is stability and guarantees, will bring much destruction.

A Two vibration needs to come into Union with the Diamond Light of Nine; to detach, to observe, to BE, to not expect that things are going to be a certain way, but know they are going to be as your Soul has chosen, your Destiny, your true Destiny of experience and exploration. For an explorer does not sit at home in the safety of four walls trying to keep change from knocking at the door; an explorer is out there flowing, travelling, moving, accepting, discovering.

A Two Gift vibration must embrace change. Embrace change, embrace growth, embrace the natural rhythms of the Oceans of Huemanity. Immerse yourself in the Waters of Life, meditate near a babbling brook or a slow-flowing stream. Feel yourself becoming one with the flow of the water, becoming one with the Diamond Light of Nine, your Higher Self, your all-knowing Self. This will then give you the Trust to change and flow. For change and flowing with that change is, in Truth, your only foundation.

THREE GIFT VIBRATION

As we now explore the gifts and the challenges of this Diamond Light of the Three, it is important for you to remember and to know that each of these Gateways of Light is in direct Union with the Planets that we express to you now. It is a direct link to the vibration, the love and even the personality of the Sun, Moon and Planets. They are Gateways to exploration of your Universe and Self Discovery of You. Much shall be shared with you in future Scriptions of these Guardians and Beings of Light that encompass you and your Earth.

These Three vibration Beings come here to express themselves as catalysts for many other beings. The Three vibration is often misunderstood, often ridiculed, often seen as different, bringing them confusion, doubt and fear of their gift, of their path and of their Truth. They are the initiators, the spark-lighters, and the doers.

Often a Three vibration would have experienced at least one past life cycle with some form of serious physical affliction, bringing restriction and lack of expression to that life cycle.

A Three vibration has a great need for expression, to create; however the challenge for the Three vibration is to be able to detach from the fear and the doubt of others; to not allow others to condemn you, for this is the ultimate source of your confusion. The Gift, the spark that you carry to create, needs to be integrated and consolidated firstly in your own life cycle, for this gives you the 'protection', the validity if you choose, to be able to go and be accepted by others in creating new life, new ideas, new ways for others. As has been expressed, the Eight vibration which is coming into Union with the Three, needs to be embraced through honouring all life, all beings, and understanding that each and every being has a role to play, a part to be in this hueman condition.

This Diamond Light of Three vibrates directly in Union with your planet Mercury, often symbolised as quick-silver, representing speed of thought, new ideas, the hueman mind. This hueman mind aspect needs to come into Union with the Higher Mind aspect of the Eight Diamond Light, to be integrated, to be initiated into the cycle of the Soul's journey and purpose.

For thoughts to manifest into creation they require confinement. Not unlike the confinement of a foetus in the womb, until there is no room left and the Soul must journey into a new life, a new dimension through birth.

The Three vibration's Gift to the world is expression, action, breaking through limitations and creating new pathways while embracing the challenges of others' fears and doubts. Often a Three vibration will incarnate into restrictive conditions and could have experienced physical difficulties at birth, which may even be carried through into adulthood. For it is through these restrictions that the energy builds to create change, create growth, create new life, a new way. For we now talk of the Union of Mercury and Saturn.

It would be pleasing and supportive to you, to immerse yourself in water, to surround yourself in the warmth of water, as that of the foetus which is surrounded in the nurturing fluids of its mother. Feel the confinement and the freedom all in one moment. Surround yourself in water; be it as you bathe in the ocean, under your waterfalls, deep within your seas. These are where you feel the safest and where you can experience the Gift that has come to express itself and from that place of confinement and freedom you will inspire and support your Soul to create, to initiate, contemplate and regenerate.

This completes the triad of your Moon. We now journey to the triad of your Sun and begin in the Diamond Light of the Four.

THE TRIAD OF THE SUN

As we arrive at the Gift of Four, we also arrive at quite a 'hotspot' in your present being, for this is where your presence of being can be found to be quite amplified and strong in its expression.

Before I express to you the Gift of the Four vibration, I wish to add that, in this Triad of the Sun, all your 'Crises' will birth themselves energetically first in your Four, then in your Five and eventually in your Six Diamond Lights.

All Crises in your life come from your denial of your Christ/Isis being, of your God/Goddess/All That Is being, as you - in you. So all Crises that you draw to yourself and create for yourself are designed to bring your attention to the Christ within and the Isis within, for that is the ultimate destiny of your Soul. And when you do not acknowledge and access the Gifts of the Christ and the Isis that are you, for they are always there as you and for you, you will find your life in Crisis.

So a new perspective needs to be placed upon this word, for it is a truly sacred word. A Crisis in your life is designed in Truth to be a sacred awakening within you, for the Christ Consciousness that represents itself as the Triad of the Sun wishes to be in Union with the Goddess Consciousness of the Moon, the Triad of which we have just spoken.

These two consciousnesses of God/Goddess, Male/Female, Light and Dark, their Union shall bring you into the ONE, into the Stars, into the Universes of the Third Triad. So see your 'Crisis' as a gift and an opportunity to access the Christ and the Isis within.

FOUR GIFT VIBRATION

To have come to the Earth with the Gift of Four is to be a brave Soul indeed; is to be a Soul willing to stand in its own Light, to stand in adversity, to stand open to persecution, to stand vulnerable and innocent, bearing your Soul, having the courage to be vulnerable, to be on show if you choose, for all to see. And, as we have expressed in other Scriptions, one of the greatest challenges for you as a Soul is to be vulnerable, which is to expose yourself to other Souls.

The challenge of being a Four vibration is that it is easy for you to be "boxed in" by other people's opinions of you, to turn the persecution on to yourself and believe the negative script you are being told by self and others.

This is why Union with your Seven Diamond Light is imperative for it is only the Unconditional Love of Higher Consciousness that can release you from this illusion of persecution and resurrect you into the state of true realization; for, remember, it is your mind that can bind or liberate you.

The Gift you share with others is enthusiasm, to be a pioneer, to stand in the light of adversity and still create Union and Peace and Joy. For this Diamond Light of Four, as you already know, is represented by your Venus, the planet of relationship. As a Four vibration there would be no half-measures in your relationships with others; they would be either all or nothing - but it takes a brave Soul to experience this. You have the Gift to resurrect a tired Soul, a Soul that's in despair. You give support and comfort and have the ability to purify any situation of negative charge. You have the Gift to see the purity of each and every Soul and the Love that lies deep within. The challenge, dear ones, is to see that Purity and that Love which lies deep within yourselves also.

As a Four vibration you would have had many incarnations standing up for the Masses, speaking for, defending and sacrificing yourself for those who could not speak or defend themselves. You have been a Crusader, and the challenge for you in this life, is not to be such a crusader for others, but to be a saviour for yourself, so that through your own grace and love of self you shall show others The Way. And we can feel your anguish as you read these words, for you are not accustomed to supporting and nurturing yourselves.

With the vibration of Venus we understand your yearning and your need for Love, however the Love of Self must first be accomplished.

We suggest that when the inner turmoil and inner criticism of Self begins to erupt, to go lie on your Earth in your Sun and see an explosion of Golden Light in the region of your Solar Plexus and Third Eye; allow these to expand and fill your entire being with Golden Christ Light. Ask for the Christ to be with you, to guide you, to heal you. Allow the Sun to fill your Soul and your Mind with Truth and Love.

Being a Four vibration does bring all your Soul's yearnings and abilities to the surface. It is a very potent and passionate vibration that needs your full expression and response, for to repress such energy shall bring many problems to your lymphatic systems and your digestive systems.

A Four vibration is extremely sensitive to the fears and doubts of others and these must not be taken on because they will affect the organs associated with the Solar Plexus. So purify yourselves with the Golden Light of the Sun and know that you have come here with the Gift of baring your Soul so that others may find the Light and guidance of their own Soul within.

FIVE GIFT VIBRATION

This Gift of the Five vibration is filled with paradoxes, is filled with parallel Universes, time lines, dimensions and beliefs. In one aspect, this Five Gift encompasses All That Is; it is the midpoint, if you choose, between Heaven and Earth, and so access to the more dense vibrations of Earth are no different to accessing the lighter vibrations of Heaven.

So as there is balance there can also be conflict, as there is harmony there can also be confusion, as there is grace there can also be disgrace, and as there is love there can also be fear.

To possess the Gift of the Five vibration is one of tremendous responsibility and one of tremendous freedom. For, understand, freedom and responsibility are one and the same thing. You have the responsibility of responding to your abilities, for when you respond to your abilities, this gives you your freedom of expression, your freedom of being, your freedom to create, your freedom to commune in Union with All That Is.

To bring the vibration of Five into this incarnation shall tell you that your Soul is ready to express Mastership. It is ready to experience the Truth, and this, of course, without a doubt can bring enormous challenges into the life cycle.

The challenge for the Five vibration ultimately is to keep their Heart open and to still their mind which will be demanding confirmation of the Gift for the benefit of the Ego. So the challenge may be one of a juggling act keeping the balance, the harmony and the grace and the love present within the experience.

When you move your experience from your Heart into your Mind, many conflicts can be created, and when the Heart and the Head are in conflict, no truth, no love, no balance and no harmony can be present. However, when you do express the Gifts of the Five vibration, it is not only transforming to you but brings transformation to All who experience you. You open a doorway to peace and love and truth for many; you radiate a warmth, an understanding and a compassion that speaks directly to the heart of the receiver. It allows the receiver of this energy to feel safe, supported and nurtured, to explore their own Heart, to explore the Eternal flame, the Infinite flame of Love and Light that is present within every Heart of every Being. And we understand the challenge often associated with experiencing that flame within your Heart, for it is so pure and filled with purpose and passion, neither the Mind nor the Will can fully understand it, and past life cycles would have seen you condemned for being a freedom fighter for the innocent or weak.

Union with your Six Diamond Light is required to guide and harness such a potent Gift, for it is your intention that will bring clarity or chaos to this Gift. Your Divine Will always has the knowledge of your highest purpose, and its intention is always pure, passionate and even playful. For, understand, your Sun in the Five Diamond Light and your Mars in the Sixth are both elemental of Fire, so bring the two into one magnificent flame of truth and love.

So for a Five vibration, solitude and a feeling of being alone may often haunt you. We understand your despair about not truly being able to express, in thought or words, what can be felt in your Heart. So, as your challenge is keeping the balance of your Heaven and your Earth within your life, your Gift allows others to find their Heaven and their Earth in Union.

To assist you with the challenge and the expression of the Gift, we ask that in meditation, or, if you choose, sitting in the rays of your Golden Sun, that you see and feel the Flame of Truth burning within. A beautiful golden flame, even a violet flame. Feel it burn deep within your Heart and know it is the flame of purpose, passion and play. Allow that flame to give you an inner experience of truth and love. And know this truth: you cannot 'think' and 'know' something in the same moment; it is your mind that thinks but it is your Heart that knows. It is your Ego that wishes for confirmation of the Heart's knowledge, and herein lies the true essence of the challenge; for only when the Ego surrenders to the Heart can the Ego know Peace, know Truth and know Love.

SIX GIFT VIBRATION

To experience the Gift of the Six is to begin to experience the mysteries of your own life, of the Universe and Beyond.

As a Six vibration, there are many obstacles put into the lifetime of the Soul and as we have said, there are no accidents. Every single event, person and thing has been placed in your lives with love, with the One intention of expansion and growth. The challenge of the Six vibration is not to resist these obstacles and not to fight them, not to struggle. There is often much struggle for a Six vibration, much despair and much confusion. But those obstacles have been placed there in Divine proportions to assist you in surrendering to the Divine Will of yourself and the One Source, to completely trust, to completely offer yourself for Service. For, in past life cycles, you have experienced the will of a tyrant, or executed some form of tyranny yourself while in the position of leadership.

So the obvious challenge for a Six vibration is to have no resistance, it is to accept. Many of you will say you have learned great patience. Patience is still, however, attached to the energy of expectation, for in patience you are waiting for something to change, waiting for something to be different and while you're waiting for that change, what you actually require is there before you, and what is before you is the Divine waiting to guide you. For a Six vibration can have a very strong attachment to earthly ways. And understand this: there are two types of logic that all of you must understand.

The first is what we call your 'Earthly Logic' which is based on the foundations of fear, illusion and doubt and all that has gone before you in Earth History. Then there is 'Universal Logic' which is based on the highest intelligence, the highest truth, and the highest love.

The two cannot be mixed or intertwined, so for the Six vibration, the challenge is to see their life and to perceive their life through Universal Logic, not Earthly Logic.

So patience, dear ones, will not be of assistance in your struggles with your obstacles; only acceptance will allow them to dissolve, acceptance and surrender to the Universal Mind and the Universal Heart. For when you do this your Gift is truly a powerful one, for you will show through surrender what is truly possible and what is truly achievable, and what Earthly Logic cannot give. The limitations and the obstacles you find in your life will disappear; you shall be set free; you shall set others free through trust, faith and Divine Will. For, we can guarantee you, to execute your fears through your Free Will, the obstacles, limitations and struggles you find in your life will only bring you more struggles, more obstacles and more limitations.

A Six vibration, for the well-being of their metabolism and for the wellbeing of their hormonal systems, must express themselves through this Diamond Light of Six. The planet for this Diamond Light of Six is Mars. Mars has often been seen as a negative planet of war or misused power, of aggressive action, and this is how we could describe the execution of the negative aspects of your Hueman Wills. However that red ball is also one of passion, of right action, of true power, of integrity, of Divine Will.

> *To assist you in the challenge and the Gift of the Six vibration, we would suggest using sound, opening this Diamond Light of Six with toning, with song and with humming. Use the powerful energetic vibration of Sound to soothe your Hueman Will to comfort, to allow it positive expression, and to also give permission to Divine Will to voice itself through this centre. Sound is the language of the Universe, and when expressed from the Heart, can be understood in any dimension, any time and any space.*

So, bringing Union to the Six and Five Diamond Lights will allow the transformational qualities of Love to be expressed through the Truth of Divine Will. So open up your Heart, open up your Soul and allow their language to be expressed through the Diamond Light of your Six, for this is your Gift.

THE TRIAD OF THE STARS

Now we journey to the Triad of your Stars, of your light, of your dreams and of your multi-dimensional Being. You are, all of you, the Stars; you are, all of you, the Light; you are, all of you, multi-dimensional Beings.

However, in this Triad of the Stars, many obstacles of the mind must be overcome and illusions must be stripped away, for only in the mind can there be illusion.

It is the last veil, the last blockage, before realisation; for, to realise Truth is to realise reality, and if you truly wish for truth you must let go your idea of your earthly realities and perceptions.

We bring you now the first Diamond Light in the Triad of the Stars.

SEVEN GIFT VIBRATION

The gift of Seven is the Gift of Sight. It is the Gift of Awakening, of Awareness, of Realisation. To embrace the Seven Gift vibration however, you must first embrace your illusions of Self and of the world around you; of everything that to this point has had an impact on your life, on your perceptions and on your reality. For, understand, your mental reality does not exist other than through the eyes of your perception.

Understand also, there is not just one realm of illusion, for within every dimension that your mind can access there is illusion attached to that dimension. However, we do not wish you to perceive illusion as a negative thing, for, like everything it has a Divine Purpose, and illusion's Divine Purpose is to protect the Truth, for the Truth cannot be bargained with, manipulated or misconstrued.

However, we do understand there are Beings who wish to do this and many have tried. So illusion is the invisible bodyguard of Truth. Many can have an insight of the Truth, but if it is not received and embraced by a pure Heart, the illusion of the Mind will step in to once more put the veils in place until the initiate realises the Truth can only be experienced with the Heart.

Illusion is the Guardian of the Truth, and to attempt embracing the Truth firstly with your mind could send many hueman beings into madness, for the Truth, in its power and in its Light, is blinding.

So, illusion plays an important part in protecting your minds, in protecting your ego and protecting your perceptions until you are ready to receive Truth. So a Seven vibration will often, for many years, be battling their way through illusion, through doubt, through confusion and through fear. But the quest for Truth would be burning very strongly in the Diamond Light of your Four, of your Soul, and Union of these two is very necessary if the Truth is to be realised for your Soul needs to guide your ego and your mind, needs to help it understand the true Gift of Spiritual Sight and the realisation that the Mind cannot understand Truth until the Heart first knows and remembers Truth. This can put much stress and pressure on the mind and the mind can find itself doing battle with itself many times over.

The Seven vibration would have spent many life cycles in meditation and in isolation. You have run the gauntlet in all aspects of the mind and you will continue to do so for at least 4 seven-year cycles in this present lifetime. Many could have found themselves in crisis or major life change around the age of 28 and often from this age of 28 to 35 there can be much mental purification through confusion and release of illusion.

Understand, the mind is only doing one of two things - it is either expanding or contracting its thought-forms, and this Diamond Light of Seven is represented by your Jupiter, the planet of expansion.

So of course, the challenge of the Seven vibration is the battle with illusion, is the battle of who they truly are, with who they think they are, or should be.

A Seven vibration can have battles with addictions. Addictions with toxic substances, addictions with thought or addiction to restrictions, bringing them into tunnel vision or limiting belief systems.

Your Light of Seven however, is one of true beauty and true insight as you have the clarity of sight for others, to see the beauty and truth within them; you know their Soul's journey and give them inspiration. You assist the Soul on its pilgrimage to Truth. You yourself are a pilgrim journeying long and often alone on a path to Truth. You now, as your challenge, must give yourself the same optimism, the same hope, the same faith and the same inspiration that you give to others. This is what will set your mind free from illusion.

We suggest, to assist you with this gift and challenge set before you, to place yourself in a quiet and dark space, to light a single candle, and with eyes closed, to focus on the pure golden flame of the candle which then fills your Seven Diamond Light. See the light burning deep within your forehead bringing expansion, bringing illumination to every recess of your mind.

Allow the illusion to be lit by the light, by the Star that sits deep within the centre of your mind. Let the warmth of the light comfort, and the flicker of the flame burn brightly within, giving support and peace of thought. For the gift of the Seven is to show the world its beauty as seen through the eyes of the Divine. Many of you require visual peace and joy, so gaze on the stars at night and the beauty of your nature by day and express yourself through art and creativity so that the mind may find peace and expansion through colour, through shape and through form. This would also relieve any blockages associated with the head and eyes which can often be experienced during your life cycle.

Allow your Divine eyes to see the love, truth and beauty that is within all creatures great and small.

EIGHT GIFT VIBRATION

As we have expressed, the number of your Eight is indeed a powerful path and to express it as your Gift is a great challenge, of which a Soul would not have chosen unless it was ready to apply itself.

The Gift of Eight is one of true, deep Soul-experience. If you are an Eight vibration you will be experiencing a very profound journey indeed. Many of you will jump to the conclusion that this is a path of a Karmic gift or Karmic challenge. However, we wish first to clarify what Karma truly is and what Karma truly is not, for until you can understand this perception that we now give you, you cannot truly embrace the profound path you find yourself on with the Eight vibration.

Your Karma to this point has been understood by many to be an action and reaction equation, or what you put out comes back to you, or what you sow you shall reap, or what you've done you shall pay for.

You have the perception of 'good Karma' and 'bad Karma'. The fact that you can call something good or bad means there is judgement attached. Unconditional Love does not perceive anything as good or bad; unconditional love cannot label an event as good or bad.

What you need to realise is, Karma is an energy that has not been given recognition. It is an energy that, through an experience, has not been fully embraced, not been fully understood. You already understand that you are magnetic, that you are electric and that you are etheric.

Unless the energy created from an experience is allowed to flow and travel through your entire Shell of Light, including your physical being, it will become magnetised; it will be held in a place somewhere within. And when it becomes magnetised it will attract to it an experience that will bring your attention to it. However, more often than not you focus your attention on the experience and not the energy that has attracted that experience. You must begin to look past the experience, for that is what you call Karma, and find the energy that is within you that has attracted the experience to it.

For that is what Karma is; it is the energy within you that is attracting to it an experience, so that it may get your attention, it may get your resolution, it may get your understanding and your recognition, so that it can transform back into pure life force, back to being of service to your Soul.

To put it another way - Karma is birthed from your Soul, and Karma is a message of direction from your Soul that the Mind has refused to hear, so a 'road block' or 'diversion' on the path of the Soul is created until the guidance is received by the Mind and executed by the Heart.

Your Soul has memory of all its experience, your Soul has memory of the reactions and the energies those experiences create, so, understand, as we talk of the Eight Gift Vibration, we also talk of your planet Saturn, the planet that you have called Father Time. Understand, in your Kabbalistic teachings, Saturn can represent the Mother and the birth of the first form. That is why Saturn symbolically is where you first birth yourself on your journey into your Universe and the Hueman experience, so it is a number of great power and great purpose.

So, the Gift of the Eight is to give divine insight, to give deeper understanding and compassion to assist others in breaking free of their patterns and habits and the energetic chains that bind them. An Eight vibration has experienced many mental, emotional and physical conflicts in past life cycles, which are now lodged in the physical body, and predominantly in the skeletal system.

An Eight vibration needs to aspire to higher thoughts and higher ideals as you have the gift to show people a new way, a lighter way, a pure way for the path of their Souls.

The challenge for an Eight vibration is not to condemn or restrict yourself, or to discipline yourself to the point of crippling yourself with those disciplines and those expectations.

For we understand the shock of a Soul taking on a hueman form, for the restriction and the discipline required is great, for it feels as though freedom has gone, movement has gone; however, this is not so, but often an Eight will feel they are condemned by being put into a human body. have been put in a hueman body by your own Divine Will, for you wish to experience the intensity and discipline of the hueman experience.

We suggest for the challenge and the gift, your union with the Three Diamond Light, that centre of birth, of creation and of initiation; for know that you can initiate many new things that will set you free from the inner chains of what you call your experience of Karma.

We also suggest that you stand under the stars and imagine expanding yourself and become those stars. Visualise the Universe in your Shell of Light and see yourself in the centre of your Shell surrounded by stars, and let this light fill your whole being bringing you once more into Union with your Higher All-Knowing Self for you are here to inspire others to become the Stars they truly are!

NINE GIFT VIBRATION

We now bring you to the last, but not least; to the Diamond Light of the Nine. This Diamond Light of Nine will bring the experience of many energetic vibrations, many avenues of which to explore. It would bring multi-dimensional thoughts, multi-dimensional emotions and multi-dimensional experiences. For the Nine, as we have expressed, takes in all the other numbers, divides back into itself and multiplies itself, always coming back into its original form. So the 'flood gates', if you choose, are open to a Nine vibration. This understandably can bring grand enlightenment but also grand confusion, for unless the Nine vibration is in Union with the Two, the physical being, much chaos and many energy blocks can be experienced. So a Nine vibration has natural access to all things, can be all things and can think all things. Many great Minds and great Souls possess this Nine Gift Vibration. However, many are also confused, isolated and in despair.

So make no mistake; the mind and the body need complete Union if they are to harness and channel the Nine Gift Vibration. For many lifetimes before this, you have been in experience of many highs and lows, and all these experiences have led you to this Nine. The peak, if you choose, of your Soul's path.

However, all that has gone before you; all that experience, all that energy, if not understood, if not accepted within your body within your mind and within your heart, can bring all those past life experiences erupting back into this lifetime. But we say, you cannot embrace anything you cannot handle.

The Gift of the Nine vibration is one of dexterity, one of high intelligence, one of beautiful clarity and insight for other Souls.

You have the gift and the ability to place yourself in someone else's shoes, to experience first hand what they themselves experience, what they themselves think. You must, however, be very aware of the dangers of this. That is why it is of utmost importance that the Nine vibration becomes the observer, becomes detached from the hueman drama, the human script.

For, it would be easy as a Director, if you choose, of other Souls to get up on that stage yourself, to become part of the scene, part of the play, to express your thoughts and your knowing, for you wish to see other Souls complete their purpose, complete their path. For the NINE itself is completion; it has travelled through all the other vibrations of the other numerical symbols.

However, we do stress: the true Gift of the Nine vibration is to observe, is to contribute also, but from a point of detachment and observation, for you are, if you choose to put it another way, a 'psychic sponge'. It is very easy for you to pick up the conditions, as we have said, including physical, of other beings.

You possess high wisdom, but that wisdom needs to be grounded, needs to be physically activated into the diamond Light of the Two at the base of your body, for as you are the psychic sponge of physical, mental and emotional energies, it is very important that you have strength of Union with your Two Diamond Light. The Two Diamond Light represents your physical body, your physical well-being, your physical vitality, for if your physical being is run down, it cannot support the emotional and mental well-being of your body.

Uranus is the planet associated with the Nine Gift Vibration. It is represented in your Kabbalistic teachings as highest wisdom, highest ideals. As a Nine vibration we suggest that you ingest, through your mind, the teachings of the prophets, the teachings of the philosophers, so you keep your mind pure and in touch with its higher purpose.

For, understand, Uranus represents your highest intelligence, your highest wisdom and your Moon represents your subconscious and your unconscious thoughts and beliefs. So both centres need to be kept pure; your physical bodies need to be kept pure; your emotions need to be kept pure; as do your thoughts, for contamination of your bodies, your minds and your emotions is the one aspect of which you need to be made extremely aware.

So we suggest a daily ritual of purification. You may wish after bathing to anoint yourself with essential oils. To keep your space of sleeping energetically pure, with incense and with candles. To take in pure breath into the body and into the mind. To Will yourself to see only the purity and the love in every being that crosses your path. For, if you can do this, the gift that your Soul provides to others is the gift of purity and love, is the understanding, the wisdom and the guidance required by all Souls at some point in their journey. And you as a Nine vibration have all the ability to do this. So, Be the purity; Be the love that you already are. Honour your mind, honour your body, honour your heart, for by doing this you can give those same gifts to the Souls that are so desperately in need of remembering their own purity and their own love.

RAINBOW SERPENT EXERCISE

An exercise that we, the Union, know is very beneficial to your Whole Hueman Being is to bring your awareness, your 'inner-eye', to the Diamond Light of Ten and see being birthed from that most magnificent point, a beautiful spiral of Rainbow Light and, as from the perception of your mind's eye, knowing this Diamond Light of Ten that rests approximately 48 cms (18") above the Crown of your Head, see this Rainbow Beam of Light be birthed from the Diamond Light of One Zero.

See it gently flow down the right-hand-side of your body and feel it travelling through the Diamond Light of your Heart and as it does, allow it to fill your chest with multi-faceted beams of Rainbow Diamond Light.

As it continues through the Diamond Light of your Heart it brings itself out into the Light Field of the left-hand-side of your body and travels down under your feet to the Diamond Light of One. Now see this Diamond Light of One become a beautiful ball of Rainbow Light and see this Rainbow Light reach down deep into the Heart of your Mother Earth, sending her love and light for her journey.

Allow this beam of Rainbow Light, this Rainbow Serpent of the Mother manifesting herself into the sacred form of the Father, to then ascend gently but forcefully through the right side of your light field returning to the Diamond Light of the Heart crossing over itself and bringing Union to Itself. And see it draw itself back up along the left-hand-side of your body;

see it ascend now back into complete Union with itself, back into the Diamond Light of the Ten. Repeat this exercise eight times.

We suggest with your willingness for balance, harmony and increased well-being, that you practise this exercise as much as you desire, for it will truly bring you immediate balance and immediate Union with yourself, with your Heaven and with your Earth.

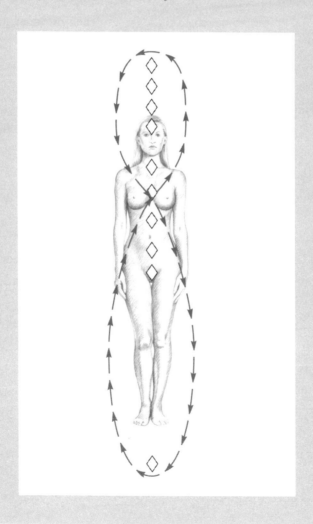

THE LOVE OF FEAR

Each gift that has been expressed to you, is a gift within each and every Heart and each and every Soul. So, you may remember knowledge, truth and peace by embracing each of the gifts and each of the explanations of the gifts.

However, we wish to express something that in your time of history has been grossly misunderstood.

As we have said, we do not dispute your journey to this point, for all is Divine and all is perfect, so the experience of Fear has also been Divine and perfect, however, Fear is now giving you the opportunity to release it, so you both may be set free.

For, understand, Fear holds within it Love, Truth and The Way back to the home of your Hearts and your Souls.

For Fear in its purity and its essence is guiding you back to The One, to God/Goddess/All That Is, for without the experience of Fear you could not possibly know the experience of Love, Inner Security and Peace.

Fear now wishes you to embrace it, to acknowledge it and give it gratitude, for, like you, Fear is returning home to its Source. Fear has sacrificed its own experience of Love and Peace to show you The Way. Fear has been of the greatest service to every Heart and every Soul.

This must be understood now, for when you keep Fear as your enemy and not your friend you cannot possibly have Union, you cannot possibly experience Joy, Truth and Love.

Over many, many, many, life cycles you have been taught to push your Fear away, to squash it down, to deny it.

Fear has been the guide for your Soul to tell you when you are not in

Union, to alert you to the possible disconnection you may be creating with your Hearts,which then in turn creates the energetic blocks of Karma. So many have misunderstood their Fear.

What you have been doing is pushing away the greatest friend, the greatest guide you could have, for Fear has only been there to alert you, to make it clear to you that you are losing your connection with your highest guide, your highest truth, and your highest purpose. To take this one step further, and we do take this step very delicately, for we understand the mind can and will have trouble with the following perception.

The idea of your Lucifer, the fallen Angel, the one who you were led to believe turned his back on God, this in its purity and its truth is the identity of Fear.

The energy, the essence you call Lucifer or the Devil, sacrificed itself for the higher good of huemanity. For Lucifer the energy of Fear has, in its purity and its wisdom, mirrored back to you your own fears and the disconnection and separateness many of you feel deep within your Hearts and Souls.

He has guided you back to the Source, for in experiencing such Fear and what you call such evil, He has assisted you in turning yourselves towards the Source, for that is His highest purpose and His grandest service.

So do not fear this Devil for He has been your friend; He has been the guide of all of you, no matter what race, colour or creed.

He of course comes under many disguises and different names, but still the purity of the essence, the truth of Fear, the truth of the Devil, is one of unconditional love and divine purpose for the path of Huemanity.

Written in your Biblical text the number of the Beast was the Triple Six; however, the Six in these teachings shows you that it is the Diamond Gateway, the essence of your Free Will and Divine Will.

Your Free Will has experienced fear as a negative expression or aspect, your Divine Will however, knows better and realises that it is a very positive expression and guide.

So, taking your minds back to the Sacred Triad, the three Temples of the Diamond Light System that lie deep within your bodies, you shall find that within each of these Triads, the numerical symbols will add up to Six, the same number that you have marked your Devil with. For, understand, as you are the Holy Trinity, anything multiplied by a Three will create that thing. Pure creation as we have expressed to you is in the Diamond Light of your Three.

Your Triple Six however is not the number of your greatest enemy, it is, in truth, the number of your greatest friend.

And as you add these three sixes together, you will receive the number One Eight, which then brings you to the number of your Nine, your higher self, your perfect angelic form, that creates itself into a Holy Trinity. This we understand; this teaching may bring much confusion to the mind and the body; however, listen to these words with your Heart and Soul and you shall know that it is Truth, you shall know that it is Love, and then you shall experience the Joy of the Truth and the Love of the Knowledge.

We cannot express to you how grateful we are for you to even read these words.

Understand that Truth will activate you on a cellular level, it will initiate you on a Soul level and it will transform you on a Heart level.

So, if and when you are ready, ask the sacred light of Fear to be with you, to guide you and to assist you.

For when you embrace Fear you transform it back into the pure Love it has always been, and, as we have said, Fear now is going back to the Source, back to The One for it is not required in your evolution anymore.

So embrace your fears; thank your fears so that they may be set free and together you may come back into Union with the blessedness and the Love of The One.

UNION OF LOVE
AND LIGHT

We, the Union of Love and we, the Union of Light wish to expand upon and create for you a deeper understanding of our existence and our position in your Universe. We know your mind loves to play games, so we shall play one with you now. We shall ask you to look at your word UNION and to break it into two parts, as set out before you.

un-ion

As we have already expressed to you, the 'ION' aspect is the electrical charge that expresses your lightning, which does also express the power of light within your Universe. It is also the Force of Will; it is representative of, and spiritually, the visual experience of Divine Will.

The symbols of the 'UN' in your hueman reality, represent symbolically your United Nations, and as your United Nations is representative of the hueman guardians and peacekeepers of your Earth, so too this 'UN' symbol in our expression is our United Nations of the Stars, of the galaxies, of the gateways and vortexes that make up this the Uni-verse (the One song, the One expression of the One Source).

For we understand your need to identify with us other than as Love and Light, for as you are realising, Love and Light have no boundaries nor do they take on only one form of expression.

So the Union of Love and the Union of Light is the Union of many Star Nations that exist in this, your Universe.

However, to simplify this concept, we wish to introduce to you five particular Star Nations that are working lovingly and purposefully with us in the expression of these Scriptions. For, understand, these Five Star Nations that we now speak of are the true ancestors of your Earth, are the forefathers of your Earth and are the Star brothers and sisters of you.

So, understand, there are two symbols that these Five Star Nations are represented by: one is the five-pointed Star and the other is the Hueman Hand. Know that before you became so involved in your minds you were very evolved in your Hearts and your Souls, and you understood that everything was connected and that everything is a symbol of everything else.

Your Aboriginals, they saw the sacredness of the hand and its five fingers, for they knew it represented the Five Sacred connections, if you choose, with the Five Star Nations, that assisted in the creation, the guidance and the enlightenment of this planet Earth, of this ball of Love and Light.

So the very first Hueman symbol, if you choose, of your Stars was your Hand, and your Aboriginals expressed this on the drawing of their Rock.

So, you hold the Star of the Love and Light and Truth of your Ancestors in the palm of your hand and you walk the pathway of your Ancestors with your feet and five toes thereof.

These Five Star Nations that you are all Infinitely connected to, wish to bring themselves forward now in these Scriptions. For, understand, even if your mind cannot conceive what we are about to convey to you, your Heart and your Soul will.

The first of these Star Nations that we wish to bring to your attention is your Aboriginals; for, understand, they came through the Star Gateway of your Southern Cross and, as we have expressed, they are the original guardians of your Earth and her sacred energies.

They were here before any other Star Nation and inhabited many regions of your Earth. It is interesting to note that out of all the Ancient Civilizations that were created originally from Star Nations, your

Aboriginals are the ones who have managed to keep their myths, their legends and their truths the most protected from your Huemanity; however, this too will change and shall awaken the memory of your true origins predominately through your physical body's experience.

The second Star Nation we wish to bring to the remembrance of your Heart and your Soul, is the Star System Arcturus and the loving beautiful beings of the Arcturians, for they are the guardians of the Christ Consciousness. They are the guardians and keepers of the energy, the essence of the Golden Sun, the Central Sun, and they can connect very much with your Heart centres. Your Arcturians have expressed themselves through your American Indian civilization.

The third Star Nation which is also connected to your cellular memory, as is all the others, is your Andromeda. They have not in their essence had much to do with your hueman race to this time and have chosen to take a back seat if you will; however, they are the guardians of the Truth of the Knowledge that is now being expressed to you. They are connected to the life-force, to the fire that activates and accelerates your cellular bodies. They can be recognised as the Mayan civilization in your Ancient times.

The fourth Star Nation that wishes to come to your attention is the Pleiadian Star System; they are the guardians of your Universal History. All that has gone before in your Universe has been recorded and kept with the Pleiadian Star Nation. You shall feel them in your higher mind, your higher consciousness, for it is there they filter all the knowledge required by you as a Huemanity, to evolve and to expand. They grounded their expression here on your Earth in the Ancient civilization of your Greeks.

The fifth Star Nation that wishes to express itself to you is your Sirius. Sirius is the guardian and the protector of your Souls, it is the All Encompassing Mother, it is the birth canal of your Universe of your Souls experience into this Earthly realm. This Star Nation grounded its energy on the Earth plane through your Ancient Egyptian Civilization. You shall feel the love of Sirius through the waters of your body and through your emotions. For, understand, Spirit communicates to you through feelings and you feel the communication firstly in your Soul.

There are, of course, many other Star Nations that support and love you, that guide and nurture you, however as we have said, these Five Star Nations are very closely linked with you on a cellular, soul and spiritual level. This is Truth and this must be remembered now.

For, understand, as we are teaching you Union with your own bodies and Union with your Earth, we also need to express to you the Re-Union with your Universe and all the beautiful beings that reside within it.

For, as we have said, everything is a reflection of everything else, and it is time for you to open your minds to ancient perceptions and ancient truths, for you cannot fully evolve back to the One until this is understood and integrated into all levels of your consciousness.

The Hands of your Hueman bodies now need to receive this knowledge and when it is received with your Hueman Hands it may then be placed in your Hueman Hearts where it will come back into Union with the Sacred Star you are.

We of the Union of Love and we of the Union of Light expand in bliss and joy in sharing this knowledge with you.

Allow yourselves to open to more Truth, more Knowledge, more Love and more Light. For, understand, even in your Earthly Realm you are perceived by us as also a Star Nation, for, as we have said: the Star that lies deep within the sacred chamber of your Heart is what we resonate with and what we recognise in you.

So your Earth is also a Star Nation and you are all Star Beings. This is Truth.

With endless Love and brilliant Light, we are here for you.

THE MESSAGE OF FATHER SUN

We, the masculine aspect of your
Universe, wish to remind each and every Heart
of the importance and great responsibility
of the journey now before you.
It is with reverence, remembrance and
honour that you must now carry yourselves
infinitely further along the path of Truth.
It is your Divine Will that shall guide you
into Bliss and Joy, and it is your desire to do
so that will allow no burden to stop you.
You are all the flame of purpose and passion.
You are all the Heart of desire and joy.
So hold yourselves back no more.
For you are burning with the very Truth
that keeps your Universe existing and beating
with the One Heart.

THE MESSAGE OF MOTHER MOON

Slowly you become aware of all the love that exists within

you; you are a child of Light, of perfect Spirit and form.

Allow the ONE to reflect to you all that you can be,

without hesitation and without doubt, for your path is

to receive from Spirit and give to life.

You are the pure life-force, the life-giving blood

that has the divine ability to give life to one another

and to the un-manifest Soul.

Your innocence is your greatest gift - it is the Heart

of your happiness.

Forever you are innocent, so forever you are happy.

Happiness has never left you and nor has your innocence.

It is your lack of receiving from Spirit that allows the

life stream of your giving to cease.

The happiness of a stone does not rely on anything other

than the innocence of its existence. And its very existence then can

give the gift of support, of shelter and of foundation for life.

Realise your innocence and you will discover

your happiness, and when you discover your happiness you become

a gift to the world.

THE UNION AUTHOR

Jennifer Starlight, spiritual medium and teacher, is the mother of two teenage children and is a resident of the Gold Coast in Queensland, Australia.

Following publication of **Union**, Jennifer will present these powerful and unique teachings at 'Communion' Workshops. The gatherings will provide further illumination and understanding of the 'Union of Love and Light' teachings, including the sacred knowledge, charts and exercises, and the individual Soul's gifts and challenges for the journey ahead.

As Jennifer continues to receive new teachings from the 'Union' for further publications, these will progressively be included in her Communion Workshops.

Jennifer will also be available for appropriate speaking engagements or other personal appearances.

For further information and dates and locations for Communion Workshops contact:

Jennifer Starlight

Jennifer Starlight

To contact Jennifer

jennifer@theinvisiblecollege.com.au

www.theinvisiblecollege.com.au

THE UNION POSTERS

SIZE: A3 CELLOGLAZED POSTERS
AVAILABLE FROM JENNIFER STARLIGHT OR THE PUBLISHERS

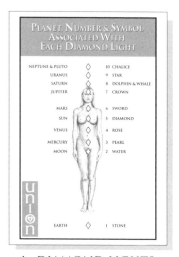

1. DIAMOND LIGHTS

2. HUEMAN PATH

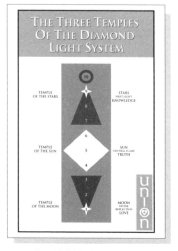

3. HOLY TRIADS

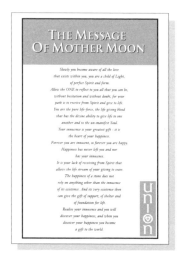

4. MOTHER MOON

NOTES

NOTES